THE
ACCOUNTABILITY
ADVANTAGE
REVISED EDITION

Play your best game

Darren Finkelstein
The Accountability Guy®

I've got a swag of happy clients; here's what they say...

So proud and so happy to be working with you.

Couldn't have asked or expected anyone better. The support you give, the guidance, feedback and kick-arse accountability are second to none.

You go above and beyond like no other. You're the best in the business and give me the confidence and belief to grow and think bigger. One of the best business decisions I made. No regrets, just big audacious goals that are getting ticked!

Thank you for everything. Can't wait to get back home and get back into it!
Mel Hird – Melinda Hird Photography

Future focused, great sounding board.
Mark Abbott – Corsair Boats

Excellent Service. Darren provides just the right amount of encouragement and gentle persuasion. Great to get insights from a successful businessperson.
Michael Hanrahan and Anna Clemann – Publish Central

Fast paced, great questions, action orientated.

Darren has a very professional approach.
Cathy Love – Nacre Consulting

Discussing my business options and directions with a like-minded individual that has 'been there, done that' is fantastic.
Christian Markgraaff – Neptune Oceanic

The Best Accountability Coach in the Game!
Andrew Griffiths – Best Selling Author, Speaker & Entrepreneurial Futurist

I got lots of good insights, it was great to talk through my plan with Darren. Feeling inspired and motivated to take action. Darren was very open, attentive and asked really thoughtful questions that helped me feel like he was really on my side.

Great sessions. Looking forward to working together further!
Clare Pyers – Pyers Health

Darren has a way of seeing clearly the pathway that I was unsure of, and laying the practical stepping stones for moving forward.
Scott Brown – Rural and Remote First Aid

No pressure, unconditional approach, validating.
Jacqui Snider – Jacqui Snider Consulting

I'm fantastic at generating the 'big picture' but when it comes to breaking that down into manageable steps that will see it come to life, well, not my strong point. And so, all these 'nice to haves' (like writing my book) go on the back burner for another time.

No BS, no excuses, just honest talk and accountability. Realistic time frames and someone to act as a sounding board who 'gets it'. If you're sick of saying you want to achieve [insert random project] and you're actually ready to step up and deliver on what you tell yourself then Darren is your guy. Very happy to chat through my experience to date. I could not recommend Darren's skill set and business acumen any higher.
Tracy Sheen – Unusual Comms

I dedicate this book to
my inspirational wife Suzi
and our two courageous sons
Jeremy and Adam.

May the road to accountability
hold you in good stead during your life.

Bite off more than you can chew
and chew like crazy...

DELIVERING WHAT YOU PROMISE AND GETTING YOUR TEAM TO DO THE SAME, IS WHAT ACCOUNTABILITY MEANS TO ME. DOING WHAT YOU SAY YOU ARE GOING TO DO IS CRITICAL IN BUSINESS. IMPLEMENTATION AND EXECUTION ARE KEY. I MEET DEADLINES, I KEEP PROMISES, I HONOUR COMMITMENTS I MAKE TO OTHERS AND TO MYSELF. ACCOUNTABILITY INCREASES MY OPPORTUNITY. I AM RESPONSIBLE, I AM LIABLE, I AM ANSWERABLE, I GET SHIT DONE. I SEE OPPORTUNITY, OPPORTUNITY IS WHERE I MAKE MONEY. I INCREASE MY EFFICIENCY BY LIFTING MY OUTPUT. ACCOUNTABILITY IS POWERFUL. SOME DON'T KNOW WHAT IT MEANS BUT I DO. I UNDERSTAND WHY ACCOUNTABILITY IS IMPORTANT IN MY BUSINESS AND MY LIFE. I KNOW HOW TO CREATE A CULTURE OF ACCOUNTABILITY. OTHERS HOPE IT WILL HAPPEN, HOPE IS NO STRATEGY FOR ME, I REFUSE TO STICK MY HEAD IN THE SAND, I MAKE THINGS HAPPEN. I GET SHIT DONE. OTHERS HEAR THE A-WORD AND SHUDDER AT THE THOUGHT OF STEPPING UP AND BEING RESPONSIBLE FOR SOMETHING. I STEP UP, I NEVER SHY AWAY. I HAVE CLEAR FOCUS, I CREATE A PLAN, I SORT PRIORITIES AND CREATE SMALL MANAGEABLE TASKS. I STICK TO MY PLAN, I DELIVER. I UNDERSTAND THE DIFFERENCE BETWEEN ACCOUNTABILITY AND RESPONSIBILITY, THEY ARE COUSINS, BUT NOT THE SAME. I AM RESPONSIBLE FOR THINGS AND ACCOUNTABLE TO PEOPLE. DARREN FINKELSTEIN 'THE ACCOUNTABILITY GUY' HOLDS ME TO ACCOUNT WHICH IS ESSENTIAL FOR ME TO BE HIGH-PERFORMING. I LEAD BY EXAMPLE, I SET STANDARDS FOR MY TEAM AND OTHERS TO FOLLOW. I WISH OTHERS WERE HELD TO ACCOUNT, IT'S A BETTER USE OF TIME, WE'LL ALL MAKE MORE MONEY WITH LESS STRESS. I GET SHIT DONE. IT'S 2020 AND I PROUDLY **TICK THOSE BOXES**

I GET SH!T DONE

www.tickthoseboxes.com.au

"You can't buy happiness but Getting Sh!t Done is pretty much the same thing."

Darren Finkelstein
The Accountability Guy®

First published in 2021 in Australia by: Darren Finkelstein, The Accountability Guy®, founder of: Tick Those Boxes
M: +61 418-379 369
E: df@tickthoseboxes.com.au   LinkedIn: Darren Finkelstein
Facebook: darren.finkelstein

Revised ediiton published in 2023 in Australia by: Darren Finkelstein.

www.tickthoseboxes.com.au
www.TheAccountabiltyAdvantage.com.au

A catalogue entry for this book is available from the National Library of Australia.

ISBN: 978-1-92300749-9

Project management and text design by Publish Central
Author photo: Kosta Iatrou (IKON Images)
Edited by Publish Central
Proudly printed in Australia by McPherson's Printing Group
Initial cover concepts by Jaden Natividad
Cover design by Peter Reardon

The paper this book is printed on is certified as environmentally friendly.

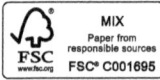

MIX
Paper from responsible sources
FSC
www.fsc.org   FSC® C001695

Disclaimer

Other titles from Darren Finkelstein
Honey, let's buy a BOAT!
Boat ownership – Everything you wanted to know about buying (and selling) a powerboat but didn't know who to ask
ISBN: 978-0-9873760-0-8

Honey, let's go BOATING!
101 bucket list of boating destinations (Victorian edition)
ISBN: 978-0-9873760-2-2

Honey, let's sell the BOAT!
Finding the right buyer at the right price
9 practical steps
ISBN: 978-0-9873760-5-3

CONTENTS

Foreword By Andrew Griffiths   xv

Introduction: The road to accountability   xvii

G'day and welcome   xxiii
The road to accountability   xxv
Interviews   xxvii

1. Identify what needs to be done   1

To succeed, you have to first set goals   4
How to set a goal: The time has come to roll up
   our sleeves and get our hands dirty   10
SMART goals   10
Big Hairy Audacious Goals (BHAG)   14
When is a BHAG useful?   16
The history and evolution of SMART goals   16
Combating the overwhelm   17
Write your goals down   21
Make an action plan   22
What are long-term, medium-term and short-term goals? 24
What happens if you fail?   25
What happens when (if) you do not achieve your goals?   30
Let me introduce you to Ned Coten   33

2. Decide it's important that you do   37

Accountability within your organisation   40
Confident decision-making   41
Trusting your gut   45
Trusting your head   47
Trusting your heart   47
Trusting your decision   48
Let me introduce you to Bruce Levy   49

3. Set priorities | 53

The Eisenhower Matrix 58
Traffic Light Method: My take on the popular method 60
Urgent vs important 63
Not knowing where to start 64
Shiny object syndrome 67
Are there any acceptable distractions? 68
How to set your priorities 74
Create and manage your to-do list 77
5D's to Get Sh!t Done – it's GSD time 79
Let me introduce you to Tracy Angwin 84

4. Plan what needs to be done and how you will do it | 89

Organisation planning 93
Measuring your progress 96
Common pitfalls and why you may fail 96
Here's my Top Seven reasons why people don't
  Get Sh!t Done 97
Let me introduce you to Rob Nankervis 102

5. Tell the world | 109

Who should you share your goals with? 113
Knowing when to share your goals 121
What could possibly stop you from sharing your goals? 122
No one cares: no Accountability Partner, no Coach
  and no Buddy 123
Let me introduce you to Anoushka Gungadin 124

6. Find a person to hold you to account 129

You can't afford to wait 136
How to find an Accountability Partner, Coach or Buddy 137
Gift a copy of this book 139

Accountability Groups (Forums or Masterminds)   140
What is an Accountability Group?   140
What can a great Accountability Coach provide you with? 144
Clearly identifiable elements and outcomes   146
Let me introduce you to Andrew Griffiths   149

7. Review process   163

Chapter 1 – Identify what needs to be done   166
Chapter 2 – Decide it's important that you do   167
Chapter 3 – Set priorities   168
Chapter 4 – Plan what needs to be done and how you
  will do it   168
Chapter 5 – Tell the world   169
Chapter 6 – Find a person to hold you to account   169
Frequency of engagement and sessions   171
What does an Accountability Session entail?   173
Let me introduce you to Chris Robb   181

8. Excuses, blame and finger pointing   191

Be authentic – you can tell when it's not real   194
Are you really accountable?   198
When there's NO accountability, it all falls to bits ...   200
My first business   200
Apple and BHP – The Big Australian   205

9. Where to from here?   209

Next steps...   212
'Free' 15-minute Accountability Assessment   213
Congratulations   215

Foreword

by Andrew Griffiths – Best Selling Author, Speaker & Entrepreneurial Futurist

What a world we live in. So much to do, so many things to distract us, so many day-to-day demands vying for our attention, our time and our energy. In many ways we've never done so much in our day, yet felt like we've achieved so little. And in all likelihood, this feeling is here to stay.

One thing I've learned over many years as a business owner, an author and an entrepreneur is that we feel good about ourselves when we make progress. That sense of achievement from getting things done helps us to feel that we are moving forward and achieving. So if we live in a world where that sense of forward movement is getting harder due to the sheer number of things getting in the way, we've got a rocky, unfulfilled road ahead. Who wants that?

This, to me, is where accountability comes into the picture – and that's what Darren Finkelstein has captured so wonderfully well in his new book. He understands all of the things that get in the way of us finishing those important projects, goals and tasks on a day-to-day basis. By knowing the villains that get in the way, we are half way to working out how to manoeuvre past them.

The Accountability Advantage provides a detailed, step-by-step process for getting the things that matter done. Whether they be big, giant projects or more simple day-to-day tasks. It's a road map for achievement, structured in a way that makes it so much more achievable.

The Accountability Advantage

Now let's be honest, there is no shortage of stuff written around this topic. So what makes Darren's book different? In my opinion, it's a fantastic combination and ode to much of the work done on accountability from pioneers in the field, combined with much of the latest study and best practice ideas, with the superglue being Darren himself. He lives, breathes (and probably eats) accountability as a way of life. And he gets a great deal of things, big things, done.

Darren holds himself accountable in every way and if he says he will do it, he does. That's why he makes such an exceptional Accountability Coach. This book is simply a written format of his own internal process. That's what makes it so practical and so powerful.

I think it's easy to assume that if you need accountability you might be lazy. What I've learned over the years is that the people who want accountability are far from lazy. They are actually the higher achievers. They simply want to achieve more and they know that one of the greatest tools they can use is accountability. That said, it's big, complex idea, one that is far more effective when we have a guide.

The Accountability Advantage is going to become one of those iconic books. I have no doubt about that. The concepts, the philosophies, the practical advice, the strategies and the real-life stories from other people who embrace the concept of accountability all come together to make this a book and a concept that really will give the reader an extraordinary advantage in whatever they choose to do.

Sit back, get comfortable, then get a little uncomfortable and use this wonderful book to get those things that matter the most done and dusted like never before. You may just find a great deal of things, many of them unexpected, change as a result of reading this book. Enjoy what's coming.

Introduction

The road to accountability

We are up to our eyeballs in the proverbial. This historic economic downturn we are facing is the toughest of our lifetime; for that we can blame this awful COVID-19 pandemic. With this has come an entirely new narrative of analysis, review and consequences.

Along the way, the world has created new buzzwords like pivot, flattening the curve and self-isolation, to name only a few. Tagging along for added impact, it seems the world has rolled out that word **accountability** once again to play. The dreaded A-word seems to be used much more frequently in the media right now. In fact, I've noticed 'accountability' gets rolled out usually when times are tough, and something's gone off the rails, such as when talking about the current state and federal politics, international politics, climate change and the state of world finances, in particular our economy right here on the home front. All these conversations and interactions prompt the discussion of: what does **accountability** really mean?

Got any idea?

Most don't, most won't agree, so don't stress. It's important before we move forward on our road to accountability to establish early the real meaning. The adjective 'accountable' comes from the Latin *computare*, 'to count'. To be accountable, a person had to 'count' what property or money had been given to him. This focus has been maintained in all forms of accountability exercised through financial accounting or budgetary records. But more discursive meanings of accountability in the sense of 'rendering account' also emerged early in the term's history.

The word 'accountability' for me is fascinating, and I feel a genuine positive connection to the word. I define it as *'doing the things you say you are going to do, and getting your team to do the same'*. Accountability offers opportunity, and opportunity is everywhere. But not everyone agrees with me; some folks don't see it the same way as I do. They see accountability as a punishment, a negative action for those not doing things right. You can blame it on the media: when they have someone in their sights as they hunt for a scalp for their front-page headline. Like the ancient Romans awaiting action at the Colosseum. Scalps sell newspapers; they also make great click bait.

For me, accountability has always been such an important element to my business. It's deeply rooted within my personal life, and is largely responsible for my business success. I can safely say that a lack of accountability is also the reason for my failures, and they've been some doozies, which I'll share with you later – and I've got the corporate scars to prove it.

The Accountability Advantage – Play your best game is the proud book title I've chosen, and it's perfectly connected with my own entrepreneurial journey. I've had the pleasure of witnessing the results firsthand which are solely attributable to being held accountable. These results mean that you can **play your best game** each and every day. The outcomes achieved distinguish and separate you from others. You take ownership, you become accountable, and with that, you take on the responsibility. You might spend days trying to come up with a solution to a problem that can cost you time and money, whereas someone from the outside looking in might see the solution in minutes.

I have worked with hundreds of successful business owners, and the one thing that they wish they had done when starting out and trying to gain some traction was to engage a coach and get support earlier. Ongoing support is a key to overcoming the obstacles that might otherwise derail you or cost you time and money. Too many people today take their dreams lightly and are afraid to put a sense of urgency and commitment to them. There's no blame, excuses or finger-pointing around here, just pure action. If you want it enough ... then you must go and get it. It's never going to come to you. If you don't believe me, then just ask others who are still waiting for it to come to them.

What an awesome opportunity we have in our lives today, and yes even with COVID. If you can master the art of full accountability you will achieve your goals and play your best game. I help high-performing individuals and teams get results, achieve their wildest dreams and smash their goals like glass piñatas. And this, folks, is what I consider to be the Holy Grail of life, both business and personal. Creating the reality you want gives you options and choices in your life. All this from simply being held to account, which in itself is not hard; in fact, with self-discipline and the creation of sound business practices with a few rituals along the way, most of us are already on 'the road to accountability' ... you just don't realise it.

I know firsthand that accountability builds opportunity, and opportunity is where I've always made money ... Increasing output is critical. Imagine you can set a goal, follow a process and 'bingo banjo' – happy days, you achieved that goal. Good on you, 'go you good thing'. Now you can tick those boxes, and get onto the next goal. Rinse and repeat, as they say. Now raise the bar just a little bit in between each goal, make it a little bit higher, and you stretch yourself to succeed and follow the process each time, and you too will be on the road to accountability and achieving your goals.

If you work through the achievement process carefully and succeed by getting the desired results you set out for with a laser-like focus, you will stand out from others when they struggle to keep up. This is the opportunity that arises from being accountable, because if you work with a renewed spring in your step while ticking these boxes of your goals, new doors will open and new opportunities will emerge.

I have always said: 'Accountability increases activity, activity increases opportunity, and opportunity is where I've always made money. Hence, the term "The Accountability Advantage".'

Along your road, separation from others is inevitable, because the cream always rises to the top. Most people misunderstand the word accountability. The dreaded A-word alarms them because it means they have to stand up and be held accountable; open to potential review and scrutiny, rather than seizing it as the wonderful opportunity it is, by embracing the positive outcomes generated by accountability. Accountability is your superpower; harness the power instead of perceiving this as a negative obstacle, holding you back and stopping you from moving forward. To many, accountability means they have to stand up and take responsibility for something. Personally, the media and politicians everywhere can take responsibility, regularly firing the accountability rocket in search of someone responsible, and demanding resignations or public hangings.

From my personal experience over a 30-year period, starting with my time at Apple, which I joined in 1992, then with my own entrepreneurial business, which my business partner and I sold in 2017, the practical and commercial definition of accountability for me is simple: *'doing the things you say you are going to do, and getting your team to do the same'*. This is irrefutable, and I often see it with my private clients that accountability is a major game changer. Get it sorted and it makes your goals so much easier to achieve and strengthens the corporate culture as a powerful tool in your company, business and organisation. In fact, sort accountability out at home and your family unit – yes, especially the kids – will benefit. This is as powerful in your personal life, as accountability allows you to retain control over what you do.

The ability to create your own opportunities is profound, instead of passively allowing life to take place around you as you sit by as a spectator. Accountability is infectious and empowers others to strive for optimal success.

It is true that if everyone keeps their promises and honours their commitments from top to bottom, holding everyone individually responsible positively helps others achieve their goals, creating a healthy and positive work culture. This breeds trust, and trust enhances productivity.

Accountability is a term tossed around in international affairs, business, economics, politics and education. Many employees loathe it because it usually means they have to shape themselves and actually get held to account. There are folks who would consider that their current activity levels see them as being 'overstretched' in their companies. Whose workloads are often set by management who largely do not even know what the A-word truly means.

My experience in business is that when something goes wrong in a company, the first question that often comes up is, 'Whose fault is it?' If there is incorrect data in the accounting, it is the accountant's fault. If we lose an important customer, it is the problem of the sales group – 'Again, they promised more than we could deliver'.

When mistakes happen, assigning guilt seems to be a natural reflex in many organisations. Even people who want to learn from mistakes fall into naming the culprits. As soon as we find out whose fault it is, we try to figure out what is wrong with the alleged perpetrator. It is only when we discover what is wrong with them that we believe we have understood the problem. They, with pointed-finger, are clearly the problem, but changing or getting rid of them (even being angry with them) is not the solution.

This common scenario is flawed; where there is guilt, there is no learning. Where there is guilt, open minds close, investigations tend to stop, and the desire to understand the whole system diminishes. Of course, when people work in an atmosphere of guilt, they cover up their mistakes and hide their real concerns. And when energy turns into excuses, blame, finger-pointing, identifying a scapegoat and denial of responsibility, productivity dramatically suffers because the organisation lacks information about the actual state of affairs. It is impossible to make accurate decisions with inadequate information. It really saddens me that most people don't know how to correctly implement a level of accountability for themselves, both personally and in their organisation, so no wonder things don't work.

Accountability isn't one thing you *do*, it's an entire way of thinking. It's the choices you make, the commitments you keep, and the knowledge that you are accountable to those in your life is central to close relationships. I often hear leaders say they want to hold their staff accountable for their actions – all well and good. But I believe this is the wrong way to think about accountability. It's not something that can be held over someone's head ...

Accountability needs to be ignited in people, and this can be done with an understanding of the wonderfully positive outcomes which can be genuinely achieved for all stakeholders: individuals, teams and management alike. If you, as a leader, create an environment where people are encouraged to do well in a healthy manner and where they are shown accountability by your own example, they choose to be held to account for their actions and for the quality of their work. That is how we as people work. Show the way, lead by example, and others will follow.

Not only does just trying to place blame not solve the problem of a lack of accountability, but pulling the trigger does not give an organisation the important understanding of why a problem occurred, what can be done differently next time, what the learnings are which can be gained, and most importantly answering the difficult question of, what can we do better next time? Sadly, no one learns from a corporate execution, and no one communicates the necessary elements required for building strong teams and resilient businesses.

The action of being sustainably customer-centric is the responsibility of a person. Some individual needs to own that task and agree to its deliverable on a date (preferably it's written into their job description) and thereby that person takes on the responsibility for making it happen.

The bottom line is: completing a goal, delivering on a promise or honouring a commitment made to others or to ourselves and making sure it gets done.

You see, there is a difference between accountability and responsibility – they're cousins, but not the same.

Let me explain. You are responsible for *things* and you're accountable to *people*.

It is essential that if we want to **G**et **S**h!t **D**one we need a person with whom we can work, someone in a central role to hold us to account.

G'day and welcome

Thanks for reading *The Accountability Advantage – Play your best game*. We'll work together through my seven modules in the road to accountability to take you on your journey towards achieving your goal, meeting a commitment and even keeping a promise that you've made to others and most importantly those that you make to yourself. Accountability has been a critical part of my own entrepreneurial journey.

In fact, when I reflect on my own journey so far, and if I reflect deeply into my 10 years with Apple, as Manager of Commercial Markets under the inspirational leadership of Steve Jobs following his return to Apple – what an era that was. What an amazing time it was to be playing in the technology industry, and accountability was right at the top of the list of things that you absolutely needed to deliver on as part of Steve's team. Having Steve on stage at a major event was actually the culmination of a series of smaller tasks, actions and mission-critical components – all of which came together behind the scenes. During my time at Apple, it was mandatory to 'do what you say' and 'get your team to do the same', and it still applies to Apple today.

Steve and his leadership team set the tone from the start and led by example in setting the bar really high, and it flowed all the way down to make sure every single Apple employee followed suit – making sure everyone played a small but crucial part in the team.

In this book, I will guide you through my seven modules on the road to accountability, which worked very well for me at Apple and then during my 15 years in my own entrepreneurial lifestyle business in the marine industry, before my business partner and I sold the business and successfully left in June 2017.

It's a process that's cemented deep into my psyche, and a framework that I still use today – just ask any of my clients in my One-On-One program.

I've built a solid reputation as someone who pumps out the activity ... I proudly GSD (**G**et **S**h!t **D**one) and I do it with passion, energy and a level of excitement which I find really contagious for others that I draw in as I work towards achieving my goals and share them with the world. I believe I've earned the title of The Accountability Guy®, a name given to me by the wonderfully inspirational Andrew Griffiths, a good friend and famous international author and entrepreneur.

I recall one summer evening in February 2019, as we sat on Andrew's balcony drinking Coronas – my bottle of happiness, not the virus – after Andrew made me dinner. Andrew said out of the blue, with no prior warning, "go and set up a business as an Accountability Coach doing what you are wonderful at – after all, you are The Accountability Guy®" ... and it stuck.

To truly take ownership of that title, I registered The Accountability Guy® as my trademark, which has just been approved. That is how my new business 'Tick Those Boxes' was born. Thanks AG xx

In fact, Andrew has been instrumental in the writing process for all my four books that I've written so far. I fondly remember back in 2012 when Andrew mentored me through the writing of my original book: *Honey, let's buy a BOAT!* Which was followed in 2014 with: *Honey, let's go BOATING!* and my final book in 2016 to end my trilogy was (you guessed it) *Honey, let's sell the BOAT!* What a thriving trilogy that was. Writing a book is a wonderful experience and an incredibly useful tool for your business, and enables you to leverage yourself as a subject matter expert and thought leader, which you are. You may as well take responsibility and ownership of that title, and put yourself out there so you can be held to account in the process. Why not?

Naturally, I wrote these books while working in the lifestyle and marine industry when my business partner Andrew Rose and I founded St Kilda Boat Sales and Service Centre, a boutique and accredited boat dealer and service centre located at the famous St Kilda Marina in Melbourne and at Wyndham Harbour, a residential and marina development in Melbourne's west.

Think about your business and your life, and I'd like you to consider all of those things which remain incomplete, unfinished, and for you remain unfulfilled in your life. NOW is the time to start delivering and make sure you get your team to do the same. This now raises my first question for you:

Do you meet the obligations, promises, goals and commitments made to yourself and others?

The road to accountability

The road to accountability starts with me introducing to you a 2010 study undertaken by the American Society of Training and Development (ASTD), which later changed its name to the Association for Talent Development (ATD). ATD is the world's largest association dedicated to developing talent in organisations. This study is an integral part of my work with private clients and forms the seven modules of our journey along the road to accountability.

The aim of the study was to determine the probability (%) of achieving a goal. There are other synonyms which can also be used to replace the word goal, they are; task, promise or commitment made to others, and above all, to oneself. The study found:

☑ 10% probability – If you have an <u>actual</u> idea or goal.

☑ 25% probability – If you <u>consciously</u> decide you will do it.

☑ 40% probability – If you decide <u>when</u> you will do it.

☑ 50% probability – If you plan <u>how</u> you will do it.

☑ 65% probability – If you <u>commit</u> to someone you will do it.

☑ **95% probability – If you have a <u>specific</u> accountability appointment with a person you've <u>committed</u> to.**

After reading this, how likely are you to achieve your: goals, promises, obligations and commitments alone?

It is this data that underlines exactly why I define accountability as game changing.

If you can reach out and place yourself in areas of discomfort and work with it, embrace it, and get through it, you WILL achieve your goals that you've set.

My goal to write this book is to ensure that you and your organisation are well-placed in the 95% zone, where goals are being smashed and your business progresses predictably towards your goal; every week, every month and every year.

Here is our exciting journey forward towards full accountability. You can follow the journey forward, which we will track at the start of each chapter.

Keep an eye out!

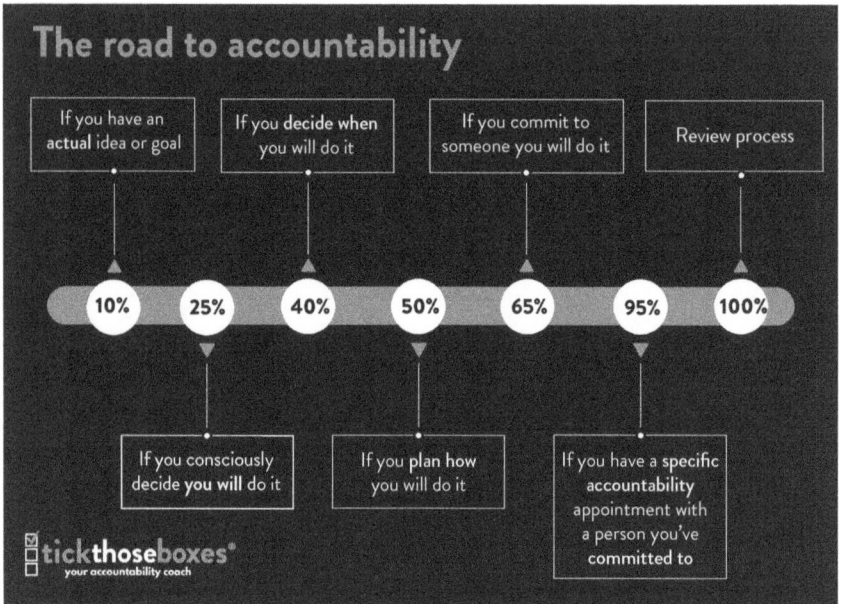

The road to accountability

| If you have an actual idea or goal | If you decide when you will do it | If you commit to someone you will do it | Review process |

10% 25% 40% 50% 65% 95% 100%

| If you consciously decide you will do it | If you plan how you will do it | If you have a specific accountability appointment with a person you've committed to |

☑ tickthoseboxes®
your accountability coach

Based on the 2010 study conducted by the American Society of Training and Development (ASTD).

In order to promote your understanding and for us to have a little fun, I have deliberately written this book in such a way that it is like a board game, which is about taking your **goal, your promise, and your commitment** from the beginning up to a 95% probability of completion, which has had a game-changing effect for me and my company.

As you complete each chapter, which is written to address each module on our trek towards 95%, you'll increase your probability of achieving your own personal and business goals, so I'd like you to keep those front and centre in your mind too.

The beauty of this process, the seven modules, is that when you move towards your next goal, project or task, you simply repeat the process from one to seven and watch your success snowball. Rinse and repeat.

Be sure to celebrate after you complete each chapter; they are genuine milestones along the road to accountability. When celebrating, the human body creates the amazing happiness chemical **dopamine**, also known as the reward chemical.

A release of dopamine is triggered when you complete a task, undertake self-care activities, eat food and celebrate little wins. Dopamine is known as the feel-good neurotransmitter

– a chemical that ferries information between neurons. The brain releases it when we eat food that we crave or while we have sex, contributing to feelings of pleasure and satisfaction as part of the reward system.

Feeling good is the driving force as you gain the necessary momentum and acceleration which will sling shot you out of the atmosphere as you focus on hitting your goals and **ticking those boxes**, in pursuit of your dreams as you **play your best game**.

Interviews

In order to further improve your learning, I have had the pleasure of interviewing a number of successful entrepreneurs and C-Suite executives and asking them to share their experiences, tips and advice in relation to accountability. We'll talk about their businesses and discuss their success.

A short excerpt of the interview questions posed to my guests is located at the end of each chapter.

Bonus video

Watch the entire video recordings of my full interviews with my guests conducted over Zoom, due to COVID restrictions and stage-4 isolation. This is available as a reader bonus and can be viewed from my website. Please visit:

www.tickthoseboxes.com.au/TheAccountabilityAdvantage

Now let's get into this...

> **'You can't buy happiness, but Getting Sh!t Done is pretty much the same thing.'**
> *Darren Finkelstein, The Accountability Guy®*

Chapter 1

Identify what needs to be done

If you already have an actual idea or goal, this is where you'll begin. This moves you to 10%.

10%

The Road to Accountability

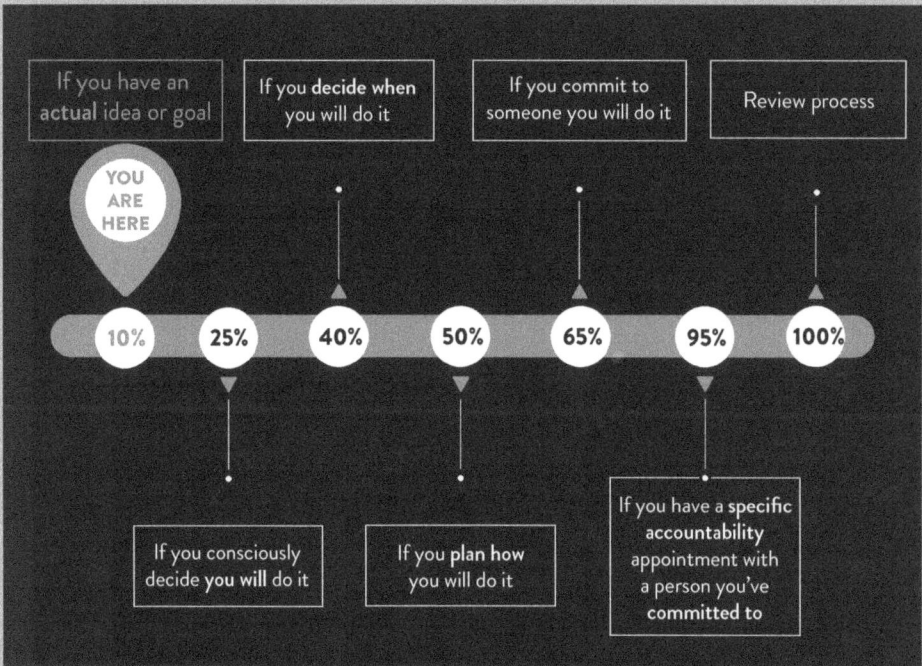

If you have an **actual** idea or goal

If you **decide when** you will do it

If you commit to someone you will do it

Review process

YOU ARE HERE

10% 25% 40% 50% 65% 95% 100%

If you consciously decide **you will** do it

If you **plan how** you will do it

If you have a **specific accountability** appointment with a person you've **committed to**

Based on the 2010 study conducted by the American Society of Training and Development (ASTD).

Before you become too concerned whether or not you are Getting **Sh!t Done**, let's rewind the clock and deconstruct, to find us back at the beginning. Now ask yourself the following questions:

1   Do I have clear-cut goals and connection to my WHY and my purpose?

2   What is it that I want to achieve?

3   Are my daily efforts aligned with my goals?

This chapter will help you identify clear goals that you can execute effectively.

We'll cover four key components:

☑   Deciding what is NOT important, and decluttering your mind.

☑   Learning to say NO!

☑   Determining your values and visualising.

☑   Designing your SMART goals.

To begin our process and to get you to your first milestone of 10% probability of completing your goal along your road to accountability, you must first identify the specific tasks that you can implement and execute effectively.

After all, timely implementation and execution are essential. And my experience often reminds me that this is a weak area for us all, usually where everything can break down.

Be introspective; looking deep inside yourself, ask yourself *where you want to be in any given time from now, say this time next year?* Knowing exactly what you want to achieve at the end of the day is a tremendous step forward.

To succeed, you have to first set goals

Without goals, you lack awareness and orientation, and you have no idea whether you have achieved what you have set out to. Like arriving in the dark in a country you have never been to ... you know, disorientation, even a sense of being overwhelmed. When you arrive, you quickly get a sense of discomfort, which is the opposite of when you return to your home country, where you know exactly what you need to do, where you need to go and how you are going to do it.

Having a clear goal not only allows you to determine the direction of your efforts, but it also gives you a measure of whether you are actually successful. A million dollars in the bank is a testament to success, but *only if* one of your goals is to accumulate wealth. If your goal is to donate money and support a charity, then suddenly it is at odds with the way you would define success.

To achieve your goals, you need to know how to achieve them. You can't just say 'I want' and expect it to happen. Creating a goal is a process that begins with careful consideration of what you want to achieve, and usually ends with a little blood, sweat, and tears to actually achieve it, and hopefully with some remarkable stories along the way. In between, there need to be some clearly defined steps that go beyond the specifics of each objective. If you know the steps for correct implementation, supported by a clearly defined plan for their execution, you can formulate goals and achieve them.

Why set goals?

I have always found that setting goals gives you long-term vision and short-term motivation. A powerful combination to fulfil the tasks you have set yourself.

Goal setting is fundamental on our road to accountability because it helps you decide and focus on what's important. Successful goal setting also lets you gauge progress and headway, overcoming procrastination and overwhelm, clearing the way for you to visualise your dreams.

If you don't know what you want to achieve, you won't know the outcome you want as a result, therefore it makes it difficult to create a plan to get you there. Goal setting is the channel that will push you to the place you want to be. Goal setting also keeps you accountable, and by holding you to account ensures you stay on track to achieve exactly what you set out to do.

Whether you're learning how to set goals at work or in your personal life, telling others about your goals makes you more likely to establish the patterns and the good habits needed to drive you to accomplish them.

Everyone sets goals, including the top performers among us, such as the world champions in their respective fields.

The world champions have carefully planned their journey to the top, they have set their goals and they have implemented and executed them precisely, only a little better, maybe a hundredth of a second better than their nearest competitor, which separates the world champions from those who are number 2.

Goal setting focuses your knowledge acquisition and helps you organise your time and resources to make the most of your life. By setting clear and well-defined goals, you can measure your progress and be proud of reaching each milestone. You will also increase your self-confidence when you recognise your own abilities and skills through achieving the goals you have set for yourself.

Setting goals connected to your purpose

Everyone has a WHY – it's the purpose, the thing or the faith that drives each of us. Goals and WHY are specific, measurable elements that ultimately serve your purpose. For example, one of your goals in life might be to enable others to take better care of the environment. A goal that will help you achieve that could potentially be as ambitious as organising a neighbourhood action to clean up the local park, or as simple as teaching your child to turn off the light when they leave the room.

You need authentic goals.

Authentic goals satisfy your needs and offer strong emotional benefits, including a sense of fulfilment, pride and happiness.

Identifying authentic goals

Authentic goals are:

☑ **Harmonious**
Setting goals for your life works best if they are integrated with one another and serve a broader purpose.

☑ **Approach-oriented**
When we work *towards* something (such as developing a good relationship with others), we have a much better

chance of sticking to it and not falling off, rather than when we work *against* it (such as avoiding conflict with others).

☑ **Centred around an activity**
Achieving activity-related goals, such as learning a specific task, meeting a deadline, or creating something tangible, can help produce feelings of accomplishment and progress, which will encourage you to keep going in the direction you're headed.

☑ **Connected to your WHY; your purpose.**
When you know and understand WHY and your purpose, you will focus much more on your goals, and this will deeply connect you and you will take responsibility and ownership – you will act purposefully, your laser-like focus will increase your determination to achieve the goals you have set for yourself.

A clear sense of purpose enables you to concentrate on the essentials and forces you to take risks and move forward regardless of adversity or obstacles.

If you have ever faced a significant crisis in your life (and who hasn't?), you will have experienced the power of destiny to tap into energy reserves, determination and courage that you probably did not know you had.

When we face a significant crisis in our lives, we all share common traits:

☑ Your mission was clear.

☑ Your goal was compelling.

☑ Your focus was laser-like.

☑ Your potential was tapped.

The purpose of the target is comparable to the energy of the sun when it is focused through a magnifying glass. Do you remember how you did that as a child, burning a piece of paper in the schoolyard? Well, I sure do.

The diffuse light is of little use, but when its energy is concentrated on a pinpoint – as through a magnifying glass – the same sun sets the paper on fire. Concentrate the forces even more, like a laser beam, and they have the power to cut steel.

Similarly, a clear sense of purpose allows you to concentrate on the essentials and forces you to take risks and move forward, regardless of adversity or obstacles.

Unlike animals, which are simply driven to survive, humans long for more than mere survival. Without an answer to the question 'survival for what?', we can quickly lapse into disillusionment, distraction, and a sense of despair.

The alarming rise in family violence, drug and alcohol abuse, depression, anxiety and suicide, as well as growing dependence on antidepressants, seems to indicate that many people in our society are in a poor state. With COVID-19 at this point in our existence as human beings, this situation has been amplified a hundredfold. The shocking reality during COVID-19 is the resulting loss of the freedom we all took for granted, including going to the cinema, attending a conference or workshop in person, attending a concert or music festival to watch your favourite band perform live on stage, travelling internationally to see the world and experience new cultures and doing something as simple as feeling the warmth of the sun on our face without a mask.

Recently, I listened to a thought-provoking and poignant radio interview with Patrick McGorry AO, an Irish-born Australian psychiatrist known for developing early intervention services for emerging mental health disorders in young people and as the founder of Headspace and the Centre for Excellence in Mental Health, Orygen and the Australian of the Year in 2010.

Patrick said the number of suicides in Australia over a three-month period for the first wave of COVID-19 (starting April 2020) was 1000, which is staggering. This compared to COVID deaths in Australia for the same period of 103.

This interview hit me hard – I found it rather disturbing to know that this exists within my community and in our own backyards, and I feel helpless and unable to assist. A quick glance at employment statistics also reveals a crisis of purpose on an unprecedented scale. I know I have digressed slightly, but given that today we are wealthier than at any other time in history, there is a clear distinction between *wealthy* and *healthy*.

German philosopher Frederick Nietzsche once said, 'He who has a why to live for can bear almost any how'. Knowing your WHY is an essential first step to finding out how to achieve the goals that inspire you and create a life that you enjoy, so that you are not merely 'surviving'.

Only when you know your WHY will you find the courage to take the risks necessary to move forward, stay motivated when the road gets rough, and set your life on a whole new, more challenging, and rewarding path. Finding your WHY has been the subject of many books and discussions. The absolute king of WHY for me – and many others – is the charismatic Simon Sinek.

Simon is an unshakeable optimist who believes in a bright future and our ability to build it together. He has discovered remarkable patterns in the way the most important leaders and organisations think, act and communicate. Simon is perhaps best known for popularising the concept of WHY in his first TED Talk in 2009, which became the third most watched talk on TED.com with over 40 million views and subtitles in 47 languages.

I suggest that you place any of Simon's books on your To-Read List. If you know and understand WHY, you will be much more focused on your goals, and that will connect you deeply and you will take responsibility and ownership – you will act with purpose, your laser-like focus will increase your determination to achieve the goals you have set yourself.

There are some well-considered questions that you should answer, like the ones I will outline later when you review your goals. This list below is for you to think about, as your answers will help you to get closer to your WHY and your objectives.

1   Where are you now?

2   What have you done well?

3   What has been frustrating?

4   Where did you make the biggest difference?

5   Why do people like working with you?

6   If you were looking at your business or your life from the outside, what piece of advice would you give yourself?

How to set a goal: The time has come to roll up our sleeves and get our hands dirty

☑ **First** think about your purpose and what you want to achieve and then commit yourself to it. Make sure they are aligned.

☑ **Set** SMART goals (specific, measurable, attainable, relevant, and time-bound) that motivate you and write them down so that they become tangible. (More about that shortly.)

☑ **Then** plan the steps you need to take to achieve your goal and tick those boxes as you complete each one as you work towards it.

The goal is a robust process to reflect on your ideal future and motivate yourself to shape your vision of this future as a reality. The process of setting goals helps you decide where you want to go in life. If you know exactly what you want to achieve, you know where to focus your efforts. One also quickly recognises the distractions that can so easily mislead one.

SMART goals

You have probably heard of SMART goals already; I love the simplicity, and make no mistake, they work – so look no further. Why reinvent the wheel?

tickthoseboxes
your accountability coach

SPECIFIC

Set Specific Goals

Your goal must be clear and well defined. Vague or generalised goals are unhelpful because they don't provide sufficient direction.

MEASURABLE

Set Measurable Goals

Include precise amounts, dates, and so on in your goals so you can measure your degree of success.

ATTAINABLE

Set Attainable Goals

Make sure that it's possible to achieve the goals you set. After all, we all want to be successful; there's no point setting a goal which is not possible.

RELEVANT

Set Relevant Goals

The goal must make sense in your life and should fit into the bigger picture of what you are trying to accomplish.

TIME-BOUND

Set Time-Bound Goals

Your goals must have a deadline, as your sense of urgency increases and achievement will come that much quicker. A due date is critical, otherwise there's no end in sight.

Like many other coaches, advisors and management consultants, I love and am comfortable recommending the brilliantly crafted SMART framework for goal setting, which was created in November 1981 by George T Doran. Thanks George.

His formula seems so simple now, but at the time it was novel and perceived as slightly bohemian by his community at large. Some thought he was a bit of a weirdo. I guess they did not understand his framework, or simply did not get its relevance to our business and personal lives.

Based on George T Doran's framework, your goals should be broken down into five aspects:

- ☑ **S**pecific

- ☑ **M**easurable

- ☑ **A**ttainable

- ☑ **R**elevant

- ☑ **T**ime-bound

Therein lies the simplicity of SMART goals, which have always worked for me. The magic lies in the letters which spell out the acronym: SMART.

Here's what it all means:

Specific: set specific goals

Your goal must be clearly and unambiguously defined. Vague or generalised goals are not helpful because they do not provide sufficient direction. Remember, you need goals that will show you the way. Make it as easy as possible for you to get where you want to go by defining precisely where you want to end.

Measurable: set measurable goals

This includes precise quantities, data and specific details in your goals so that you can measure your progress and success. If your goal is simply defined as 'generate sales', consider: how will you know when you have succeeded? If you generate one extra sale tomorrow, have you reached your goal? Without a way of measuring your success, you will miss the celebration that comes with knowing that you have actually achieved something, as a defined target tells you when you have achieved the goal.

We all need to know when we have arrived at the desired destination, otherwise you'll be striving to reach it all of the time yet have no idea of when you get there or where it actually is. 'I want to get fit,' is not a measurable goal. 'I want to be able to run 10 kilometres without stopping,' is a measurable goal.

Attainable: set attainable goals

Make sure that it is possible to achieve the goals that you have set yourself. If you set yourself a goal that you have no hope of fulfilling, you will only demoralise yourself and undermine your confidence. However, try to resist the urge to set yourself goals which are too easy to achieve.

Striving for a goal that you have to work hard at is overwhelming for some, which can also frighten you into setting future goals that are in danger of not being achieved. Setting realistic but challenging goals can determine the balance you need.

Relevant: set relevant goals

The goal must make sense with your purpose and why, which fit nicely like a piece into the overall puzzle of what you are trying to achieve. If a goal is relevant, you are much more likely to work hard to obtain it. Set widely scattered and contradictory goals, and you will waste your time and your energy.

Time-bound: set time-bound goals

Your goals must have a deadline, which also means that you know when to celebrate success. If you work on a deadline, your sense of urgency increases and you will work with more urgency. Deadlines with specific dates and times are a concrete and genuine reminder of what needs to be done and when. There's nothing like a special event coming up which motivates you to **G**et **S**h!t **D**one, and do it on time.

Personally, I love the feeling of 'impending doom'. This is what I call an event, workshop or conference with a set date, by which goals and tasks must be achieved. These dates are locked into place, there's no room for movement, no wiggle room, it's non-negotiable. It may be an event I'm professionally speaking at, as this always brings solid deadlines into play. I thrive on this scenario; it's in my wheelhouse and my adrenalin flows.

I work long hours in preparation for the event, conference, speaking engagement or workshop, so I always feel absolutely amazing when I achieve my goal, no matter the size. My goal is to deliver a meaningful experience from which my audience 'takes action' on what I've presented. My aim is to not only motivate, but to inspire businesspeople to 'implement and execute' what's needed right now in their businesses from this moment onwards.

Big Hairy Audacious Goals (BHAG)

We discussed above that **A** is for 'attainable' goals. There is, however, one exception to the rule when talking about attainable goals, and that is the inspiring and groundbreaking **B**ig **H**airy **A**udacious **G**oal, or BHAG.

This is a clear and challenging objective to which a person or organisation should aspire. A BHAG – pronounced 'bee-hag' – is a long-term goal that everyone in a company can understand and rally behind and it becomes their focal point.

Jim Collins and Jerry Porras developed and were early pioneers of the term 'BHAG' in their 1994 book *Built to Last: Successful habits of visionary companies*, which has since inspired thousands of businesses.

What is it?

The Big Hairy Audacious Goal is a statement of strategic intention – it is the specific result that the organisation will achieve in the long term (say 10 to 30 years' time).

Similar to saying you are planning to climb Mount Everest in 10 years' time, and you have developed a plan to ensure it happens. It's exciting and inspirational stuff, turning a dream into reality. It is one of the components of the 'company's vision', using the Jim Collins and Jerry Porras framework created by its founders.

What makes a Big Hairy Audacious Goal work so well in an organisation are these key elements:

☑ **It's inspiring** – it motivates everyone in the company, at all levels.

☑ **It's possible** – it's not easy, but it's doable. It is possible to achieve if the entire company 'plays their best game'. It's important for the BHAG to be real and authentic in what the company could possibly achieve – if it is set with too much ego, it is more likely to demotivate and you lose support from the team along the way.

☑ **It must be aligned** – with company strategy and the company's WHY. It matches the purpose and values of the organisation.

☑ **It must be consistent** – the BHAG has no long-term credibility if the business changes the BHAG every few years. It must be agreed and locked in concrete at the beginning.
A BHAG that is large enough will inspire, motivate and encourage teams to make a significant commitment of a decade of extraordinary effort and focus to deliver.

☑ **It must be shared** – not just created by the CEO but owned and shared broadly across the company.

Financial targets do not make good BHAGs, they inspire only shareholders, and for everyone else they are mere numbers.

In addition to the 10+ year BHAG, the company should also identify their 'milestones' – where do they need to be in at different points along the journey to be on track for their BHAG? The company can then formulate specific plans to achieve these milestones for which the role of **accountability** plays an essential role.

You'll want to know specifically:

☑ What needs to be done?

☑ Why is it important?

And most importantly, the million-dollar question:

☑ When does it need to be done by? What is the deadline and who is responsible for it?

> **'On one side of accountability is courage, on the other is freedom.'**
> *Jean Hamilton-Fford*

When is a BHAG useful?

A BHAG is a very useful and effective way of communicating a clear direction and level of ambition that will focus and unite the entire company. The management team must commit itself to the BHAG, otherwise it will not only have no power, but also lose its credibility.

Don't force it artificially – when it comes, it will immediately feel right and having someone work with you like an Accountability Coach in the long term, to achieve this goal may be the finest single investment and major difference you can make to your business and life.

In fact, what I really love about the adaptability of my seven modules on the road to accountability is that they can be easily applied to achieving your Big Hairy Audacious Goal. The principals are exactly the same, the method may change slightly. A BHAG can work for you individually as well as at work. I like to say *'bite off more than you can chew, and chew like hell'*. That's always worked really well for me.

The history and evolution of SMART goals

In the context of the history of SMART goals, the SMART methodology has only recently become a hot topic among executives. Leaders and managers are searching for a way to guide their troops to victory by laying out goals that move the company forward. To accomplish this, many have started to look toward the SMART goals approach for its simplicity and effectiveness.

Over time, SMART goal setting has helped organisations of all sizes set and achieve their objectives. The central concept is: be thoughtful about your goals.

Make them matter, ensure clarity and monitor progress towards completion. People are motivated to attain objects and things. Design outstanding goals that you can achieve ... and then turn your people (or yourself) loose on them.

In 1981, George T. Doran published a work in the November issue of *Management Review* that extended upon Locke's findings. In this work, Doran set out the main principles of the SMART goals. He recognised that companies must achieve targets and goals, but often set goals that were too wordy to have a meaningful impact.

He articulated in detail that goals are not formless, inarticulable factors, but measurable undertakings that must be achieved to move an organisation forward. He expressed the first, compelling way to define, measure, and ultimately achieve goals.

Just a reminder of what's at the heart of SMART goals:

☑ **S**pecific

☑ **M**easurable

☑ **A**ttainable

☑ **R**elevant

☑ **T**ime-bound.

Combating the overwhelm

For many people, the planning process can be taxing, both in terms of your energy and your emotions. Often, this feeling of unease arises when you think about this process. How do you feel at the moment when you think about your planning process; maybe you sense overworking or the feeling of **overwhelm**?

There is a lot to consider here – so much to think about. Many people think actually having a goal is relatively uncomplicated, but putting a clearly defined goal using the SMART framework out there isn't as easy to do as once thought. So, feeling overwhelmed right now by the task at hand makes sense.

To deal with the feeling of overwhelm, take a deep breath, hold it in for a few seconds, and release. Now breathe in again, hold, then release.

The feeling of being overwhelmed arises because you have too much to concentrate on, and you may not know how to begin the process, so you pay attention to whatever shouts the loudest at you.

Proven solutions for dealing with overwhelm:

☑ **Write it down:** Take the 'overwhelm' out of your head and put it on paper, where you can distance yourself from it a bit. You should also write down every task you can think of that you're worried about.

☑ **Bite-sized chunks:** Once you've done this, group your tasks and to-dos into larger pieces. Organising your to-dos into chunks will also help you see your world more clearly.

  ✓ Remember the old trusty quote that sums it up beautifully: 'How do you eat an elephant? One bite at a time.'

    An oldie, but it seems to make sense, and it is really a great way to work your way through a lot of stuff.

  ✓ Just take it slowly, and take it one small bite at a time.

☑ **Choose carefully:** Look at your chunks and prioritise your to-dos based on what makes you feel healthy.

  ✓ Which ones do you love?

  ✓ Which ones are you actually looking forward to?

  ✓ Make a plan to do these first, and to find a small way to celebrate completion when you've done them.

  ✓ If possible, delegate to others who may also have an interest or expertise to offer.

  ✓ People find that doing the above activities gives strength and resilience to get through everything else.

☑ **Take action:** Action is the antidote to feeling overwhelmed. Just begin. Very often the simple act of beginning will alleviate the anxiety and stress that has accumulated.

☑ **Focus:** On the task at hand. Think about what you are doing rather than what you're *not* doing.

  ✓ Worry and time have a special relationship. The more you have of one, the less you have of the other.

  ✓ Both are suspended when you simply focus on what is in front of you right now.

Many people wander through life, moving from idea to idea, and achieving nothing. How is it that some people deliver vast amounts while others muddle through life?

Is it because of magical superpowers and being blessed with innate talents and superior intelligence? NO. People achieve their goals not only through talent and intelligence, but also through what they do on a daily basis. They perform repeated actions that lead them to achieve their goals.

They are as specific as possible and outline the precise definition of their success: 'I need to lose 10kgs', instead of merely 'needing to lose some weight'. The key is to identify the **specific** measures that are needed to achieve the goal. Try to say it clearly and precisely. If you try to lose weight but do not change your diet or exercise levels, you won't achieve anything. Ask yourself: 'what will the success look like?' And if you don't know, take time to reconsider the goal.

Here's the 80/20 rule: we have all heard it. You probably have a vague idea of your goals, but they might have gotten lost among the stack of to-do lists and the day-to-day work that you're doing. Now is the time to set goals and focus on the 20% of your activities that will produce 80% of your results.

This process will help to overcome the feeling of being OVERWHELMED and possibly INTIMIDATED by the volume of things to do on your to-do list which you have set yourself that need to be completed; these items become your short-term goals.

It is about taking promises, goals and commitments made to oneself and others, and then breaking them down into smaller pieces. With this approach, you end up moving towards your goals without even realising.

Do yourself a huge favour and keep your goals honest; it is essential not to get too carried away in setting them by being OVER-AMBITIOUS.

Proven solutions to overcome this

Overwhelm typically occurs as one strives to achieve too much in an unrealistic timeframe, and cannot say NO, so they attempt to do everything.

☑ Review your schedule to see if you can actually accommodate that new deadline.

    ✓ If it places you under the pump for time, then say NO.

☑ Delegate to others, or reset the deadline, so you can fit it in when it suits you.

    ✓ We ambition addicts (yes, I'm one of those) know we have a hard time relaxing, so unscheduled time fills us with dread and the need to be actively engaged in tasks getting us closer to our goal.

Your SMART goals should not only be for yourself, but also your business.

As an example, if you are a solopreneur, perhaps one of your goals is to increase your sales. Remember: 'increasing sales' is not a goal – that is a wish, or an ambition. Therefore, a goal without a PLAN is only a WISH. You need more specific detail.

When you set goals, it's essential that they motivate you. This means making sure they are connected to you and your purpose, and that there is value in achieving them. If you have little interest in the results or if they are irrelevant in the overall picture, then the chances of you participating actively in the implementation of these goals is slim at best. Motivation is key to achieving these goals.

Set yourself goals based on the high priorities in your life, your WHY, your purpose. Without this kind of focus, you can end up with far too many goals and too little time to devote to each one. Achieving goals requires commitment, so in order to optimise the likelihood of success, one must have a sense of urgency, and it's really helpful to adopt an attitude of: *I must do this.*

If you do not have that, you run the risk of postponing what you have to do to make the goal a reality. This in turn leaves you feeling disappointed and frustrated with yourself, both of which are demotivating – you can end up in an undermining 'I can't do anything' or 'I can't be successful at anything' frame of mind.

Tips

- ☑ To make sure that your goal is motivating, write down why it's valuable and important to you.

- ☑ Ask yourself, 'If I were to share my goal with others, what would I tell them to convince them it was a worthwhile goal?' You can use this motivating value statement to help you if you start to doubt yourself or lose confidence in your ability to actually make the goal happen.

Write your goals down

The physical act of writing down a goal places it in the forefront of your mind and makes it tangible. There will be no excuse for forgetting. As you write it down, use the word 'will' instead of 'would' or 'could'.

To give an example, 'I will cut my operating costs by 10% this financial year,' not, 'could I cut my operating costs by 10% this year?' The first target statement has power and you 'see' yourself reducing costs – you take ownership. The second one lacks passion and gives you an excuse if you fall short.

Studies have shown that people process visuals about 60,000 times faster than they can imagine. You no longer need to convince yourself why it is important to write down your goals. But if that is not enough for you, there seem to be other reasons to clear up any doubts, as demonstrated in the sections below.

Tip

- ☑ Place your goals in visible places to remind yourself daily of what you need to do. Put them on your diary, wall, desk, inside your car, computer monitor, bathroom mirror or refrigerator as a constant reminder.

Written goals boost motivation

The daily visualisation of your goals serves as a positive reminder and motivator. If your goals are hanging over your desk or as a screensaver, you are more likely to be reminded to get up and get things done. If you place a level of importance on the goals, they are raised in significance. If they are important to you, they will be important to others, so please share your written down goals with others who are important to you. A constant reminder gets the message into your brain and allows you to create good habits which can be repeated with frequency, and this building of habits is where you repeat good processes which can be used over and over in the rich pursuit of your goals.

Written goals reduce stress

As I said before, as soon as you start writing things down, your head declutters. It also provides clarity and relieves you of the burden of rethinking your goals. We often get stressed when things that are important to us seem to lack clarity, and you've missed getting a genuine understanding. Therefore, your anxiety levels increase, as does your blood pressure and your stress levels. Write it down, and make sure it's unequivocal.

Written goals allow you to track your progress

Finally, writing down your goals allows you to understand where you are at in the progress towards your goal and where you need to be.

Tips

- ☑ To-do lists are great because you can identify, track and measure the progress of your goals. Written down goals are a daily reminder of your progress, and allow you to see what else you need to do.

- ☑ Ensure you add the 'due dates' next to each item, so you can keep yourself on track. Placing each of these goals in priority order will help you work out what needs to be completed first, but more about setting priorities in chapter 3.

Make an action plan

This step is often overlooked in the process of setting goals. You become so focused on the result that you forget to plan all of the steps that are necessary on the way. By writing out the individual steps, and then crossing each off as you complete each one, you'll realise that you are making progress towards your ultimate goal. This is especially important if your goal is significant and demanding or a long-term goal.

Stick with it!

Remember that the goal is a continuous activity and not simply a means to an end. Build reminders to keep yourself informed and establish regular time slots to review your goals. Your end destination may remain comparable over the long term, but the action plan you set for yourself along the way can change significantly. Make sure the relevance, value, and necessity remain high.

A valuable reminder

Goal setting is much more than simply saying that you want something to happen. If you do not define exactly what you want and do not understand why you want it from the start, your chances of success will be greatly reduced. By following the SMART process, you can set goals with confidence and enjoy the satisfaction that comes along with knowing you achieved what you set out to do.

So, what will you decide to accomplish today? Let's go with what we talked about at the start of the chapter – *increasing sales*. However, that's not specific, is it?

So, let's word your goal using the SMART goal principles. It would be: 'Increase the unit sales of the ABC product line by 20%, which equates to $100,000 and you wish to complete this by 30th June next year'.

That's better – now we have a genuine SMART goal right here, which clearly meets all of the recommended criteria. How much better worded is that to now get our heads around?

- ☑ It's specific.
- ☑ It's measurable.
- ☑ It's attainable.
- ☑ It's very relevant.
- ☑ And most importantly it is time-bound.

This is a task you are directly responsible for, and now you can take ownership of achieving that goal. With clarity, you have a 10% probability of achieving that goal using our road to accountability framework.

Let's get a move on as you follow my modules, and you'll get to 95% probability of achieving that goal on your journey towards success.

What are long-term, medium-term and short-term goals?

There's much conjecture surrounding the definition of long-term, medium-term and short-term goals. **Short-term goals** are something you want to do in the very near future. The near future can mean today, this week, this month. A short-term goal is something you want to accomplish soon. A short-term goal is a goal you can achieve in 30 days or less.

A **medium-term goal** is one that can be achieved within a 90-day period, which is a full business quarter.

Lastly, we have a **long-term goal**, which is something you want to do further in the future. Long-term goals require time and planning. They are not something you can do this week or even this quarter. Long-term goals usually take 12 months or more to achieve.

- ☑ Short-term goals can be achieved in 30 days.
- ☑ Medium-term goals can be achieved in 90 days.
- ☑ Long-term goals can be achieved in 365 days.

Tips for setting good short-term, medium-term and long-term goals

What I have always found beneficial for my clients is to discuss and answer these five great questions when we are goal setting or reviewing past accomplishments, typically looking back at the previous financial year's results, as a review.

Back at Apple, we used these same questions to discuss, review and set our sales targets for the months, quarter and year ahead.

Here's five central questions, critical in the planning process of setting your goals:

☑   Where exactly are you now?

☑   Where do you want to be?

☑   What's been stopping you?

☑   How do you want to get there?

☑   Why is it an absolute must?

I love to deconstruct as much as I can, working backwards from the desired outcome to the beginning. Think about what you want to achieve, then plan the steps necessary, taking you right back to the very start, along with adding dates by which things must happen. These milestone dates are critical, and set the tone for the importance of the goal and assist with setting your priorities.

Give it a try. Use these questions yourself and let me know of the outcomes that were achieved.

What happens if you fail?

Make no mistake – failure is inevitable at some stage in your pursuit of what's important to you, and I've devoted an entire chapter later to not hitting your goals.

'Sandbagging' is a term that refers to you setting too easily achieved goals and/or setting them so they don't stretch you anywhere near enough. Easily reached goals do not achieve anything in the long run other than satisfying your ego in the short term, but that is all. You are just cheating yourself and cheating your business.

Let's face it, we are humans with emotions, we have different personalities and with varying sized egos which form our unique DNA. With all these differences, we are therefore going to fail from time to time, so it's not a matter of if, but when?

In 1980, I remember clearly when I failed for the very first time in trying to reach my sales goal. It was my very first sales job at the youthful age of 18, working for Remington Office Machines as a sales cadet. My CEO was the late Ronald W.

Turnbull. Ron, although we were not allowed to call him that as his preference was Mr Turnbull.

Mr Turnbull was a wonderful man; he was a tough, old-school CEO, but he became my teacher, mentor and my dear friend. Mr Turnbull taught me the finer details in the 'art of sales' and in the ABC of selling, which he said stood for **A**lways **B**e **C**losing.

I clearly remember Mr Turnbull; he left his mark on my psyche. He filled me full of optimism, hope and resilience, and taught me to accept no less than seven NOs from my prospects before I backed off.

There's how to build perseverance, persistence and resilience, and in one fell swoop.

Mr Turnbull stopped me in the corridor of our office and said these wonderful words, which I will never forget.

'Hey Finkelstein, head up,' Mr Turnbull said: *'You are not judged by the amount of times you succeed, but rather by the amount of times you fail, and keep trying.'*

'So, lift your head up, think about why it didn't work for you this time round, and for god's sake, do it differently tomorrow when you WILL try it again – got it?'

'Got it ...' I said, to Mr Turnbull's delight.

In fact, I GOT IT so deeply it's firmly entrenched in my mind to this day – that conversation has carried me through the roller coaster of my life, and held me in good stead. Thanks, Ron ... oops ... sorry, Mr Turnbull.

How amazing was that advice? Such simple, wonderful and poignant words, which make so much sense. A bit like getting back on the horse or the bike after you have fallen off. Mr Turnbull, thanks for giving me so many opportunities to redeem myself – it is really character-building stuff, for which I attribute much of my own resilience, my drive and my laser focus.

And to think here I am again still drawing on Mr Turnbull's gold, some 40 years later. Bless him.

We do know what happens when we fail to achieve our goals; any one of the following or even a mixture of all:

☑ You start avoiding setting big goals because you don't want to fail.

☑ You start talking of being practical and the need to set achievable goals.

☑ You get upset and demotivated.

☑ You start losing faith in yourself.

☑ You start feeling that you are a failure.

☑ You switch over to 'why' mode and analyse what went wrong.

What could have been done to avoid failure?

What changes must you make in your planning or action process, so that your goals remain meaningful and challenging AND you really achieve them?

Of course, there is nothing wrong in failing. It happens to everyone some time or another. Look at my younger self, 40 years ago. But you cannot start on the journey towards your goals if you start with negative thinking like this. That amounts to planning to fail and self-sabotage.

The focus has to remain on succeeding with a positive mindset, precisely as Mr Turnbull said: *'Head up, Finkelstein'.*

Success and a feeling of achievement is not an ordinary feeling; for me it's one of the most satisfying in my lifetime, and to think if you achieve regularly, then you get that feeling on a regular basis. For me, that natural chemical release is way better than drugs or alcohol.

All that said, you must understand and learn from your mistakes, weaknesses and shortcomings. We all have them.

For me personally, I accept my limitations. I know exactly what I'm not so good at and I have learnt to maximise my strengths and minimise my weaknesses. As I see it, there can always be some concrete plan to pull you forward, someone to assist you in the weak areas where you need a lift and some extra support. With the right mindset, you will get by. For me, I just know from deep inside that I will always make it.

Those who set mammoth targets certainly go beyond the obvious of what you can achieve with what you already know and do. Considerable stretch targets force you to think outside the box. Obviously, extraordinary results cannot be achieved with just ordinary actions.

It goes without saying that you have to move outside of your comfort zone while chasing mammoth targets – the BHAG. So, in fact, it is the fear of the unknown over there that scares you!

Mammoth targets are always going to be scary. It is natural to feel uneasy and apprehensive about them. That's why I love achieving the smaller, more modest targets first, in the lead up to the bigger ones. I've seen many clients start with a need to build up a few little wins first, thereby gaining natural momentum, which increases enthusiasm and self-belief, and this positivity pushes you just like a slingshot, so when you build to the stretch of a larger goal, you are primed and ready to attack it head on. For some people, the failure of falling short of a mammoth target means embarrassment, frustration, loss of face, loss of respect, disappointment and reinforcement of an already low self-esteem. Big enough reasons to avoid those mammoth BHAG targets – big enough reasons to look for smaller targets. It is also true, however, that unrealistically high targets without backing of genuine action plans can never motivate you to perform. Striking a fine balance between the stark reality of the present and aligning your thoughts, choices and actions towards a mammoth destination in the future is the key. Get motivation from the distance you have travelled so far to inspire yourself to bridge the gap when you have fallen short. Motivation to achieve and will to succeed are prerequisites in this journey. The real success will come through creative thinking, meticulous planning and a load of hard work.

So, think BIG, plan BIG, achieve BIG, for BIGGER happiness and a supreme feeling of satisfaction in your business and in your private life.

A great exercise for goal setting

Imagine …

You are talking to your life partner or business partner, and you are both projecting what goals and outcomes can be achieved in the following five years.

In five years, you are sitting together to celebrate your success (whether in business or in private), and you are reflecting on those magic key moments and highlights that bring a giant smile to both your faces and that helped you achieve your goal …

As you make a champagne toast to each other, think about what remarkable achievement(s) were reached which you would be celebrating. Think about this imaginary setting in terms of SMART goals, and seek to deconstruct the goal you have in mind by working it out backwards and reverse engineering from the outcome back to the planning.

Together you define the answers to these questions and write them on the back of drink coasters or napkins.

What will your answers be?

☑ **Specific**
What is it specifically that you have done?

☑ **Measurable**
What were the measurable goals you have achieved?

☑ **Attainable**
What was that attainable goal you've just nailed?

☑ **Relevant**
In achieving that goal, why was it so critical to you and your partner in terms of the big picture?

☑ **Time-bound**
Did you meet the deadline? Exactly how accurate was the due date you placed on that item in comparison with your actual completion date?

Forward planning is key when you are goal setting. The prioritisation of your goals also encourages forward planning and a focus on anticipating what must be done.

With this focus will also come less stress, as you are better prepared and clear on what work you need to complete by when. Having concrete goals in place will serve as a guide in the decision-making process.

Remember: set goals that are SMART – specific, measurable, attainable, relevant and time-bound.

Some set 'HARD' goals, but make sure they will work and that they are truly attainable (low-hanging fruit is not considered as 'hard goals'). When setting goals for work, it's important to involve management and employees in the target-setting process so that they become more committed to achieving the goals. They will take more responsibility for the goal and concentrate on achieving it if they are involved in setting it. It is important to include these goals into your individual team members' job descriptions (if you have a team). Assign them as part of their key performance indicators, which will make them take on the responsibility for the actual achievement of the HARD goal.

As an added incentive to your team's package, there is nothing greater than the financial reward for having achieved the goal successfully. And when the goal is reached, you have to celebrate with your team.

It is a powerful team-building exercise to celebrate victories with the team. Of course, it has to be your shout, so be ready to take over the tab.

The next time the team will be prepared and ready to pursue a different goal, which you should set a little harder, and with a little more stretching the next time. Whatever you do, write the goal down and spell it out clearly, so that there will be no misunderstandings. Clarity is paramount, and will ensure that there are no excuses when things go wrong or veer slightly off track.

What happens when (if) you do not achieve your goals?

Penalty or consequences

I don't want to be negative, but I feel compelled to address the elephant in the room. When you are setting out to reach a goal, whether it be monetary, personal, strategic or otherwise, it is important to ensure that your goals are as clear and as specific as possible. SMART goals will sort out if your goal is overly vague or too broad, which will not give you the focus you need.

I also recommend when goal setting that you ask yourself a series of questions about what occurs as a result if you DO NOT achieve your goals.

What are the consequences, some people call it a penalty, for not meeting your goals? This serves to reinforce your motivation if the consequences are particularly detrimental. The consequences for not achieving your goals are the missed opportunities to learn and grow. It also calls into question your integrity; namely, doing what you said you were going to do. Not going forward forces you to remain stagnant.

The incomplete goals that were set for last year still have a chance at being accomplished, but only with very focused and intentional action. Which is why it might be time to bring on the punishment as a process agreed in advance if your task or goal is not completed on the date which has been agreed. This, after all, is the responsibility you took on to achieve your task or goal in the first place, for which you are now being held fully to account for completion. This is total accountability, and your destination for the journey you've chosen.

In setting goals over our lives, there have been a lot of rewards attached to success from as far back as anyone can remember. Whether it was a lollipop after seeing the dentist when I was a child (isn't that ironic?), or a big red tick at the end of a week in my primary school exercise book, getting positive reinforcement is something all humans respond to. However, with self-esteem building gold-star successes we have as we get older, there are rarely consequences attached to failure.

I guess the notion of not achieving the task or not hitting that goal is penalty enough, and I question that. It seems the entire world only perceives consequences being reserved for deliberate wrongdoing. In your company, there need to be consequences that are aligned with work regulations and a documented process for dealing with team members who do not achieve what is asked, such as being issued written warnings and correct protocols for those who do not achieve their key performance indicators (KPIs) on a regular basis. The worst-case scenario must surely be that that the person is dismissed and replaced by someone who can do the job, as it's costing your business money and wasted opportunity. Penalties at the direct opposite ends of the scale can also apply, and must again have a place which is documented within your process and aligned with work regulations.

I have found that having a punishment in place for not achieving a goal and making it 'adult' enough, so it's actually fun, works really well too.

Providing that it causes some level of 'hurt', not pain hurt but rather an inconvenience or discomfort as a consequence of your failure, it is a far stronger motivation when the pain of failure alone isn't enough of a negative consequence to keep you going even when you don't want to.

Here are two consequences or negative reinforcements that have worked for me during my client sessions.

What makes this work so well is that no one gets hurt, it's fun and it can be costly. The client sets these consequences themselves; it's their idea they came up with. They monitor their own progress against their goal, all in order to not have to implement these penalties, so failure is not an option and everyone wins in the end if negative consequences are not required. That is exactly why they work so incredibly well.

Consequences with meaning and a good laugh

For the non-achievement of a specific task or goal by the agreed due date, you can:

☑ Make a donation of, say, $100 to the political party that you would least support, and definitely will not vote for, which I call 'hurt money', so you do not want to lose because you will feel the *hurt* of having to pay out. Choose the party which really upsets you the most by their lack of vision and values, and who are diametrically opposed to your beliefs and values.

☑ Say you follow a particular sporting team (let's say football) and you have to stand in a queue of the team which you and/or or your family dislikes the most wearing your team's jumper and you must physically buy a season membership ticket from the team you dislike. Not only will this cost you at least $200, but you will be seen in public and possibly embarrassed by the opposing supporters. This is a doozy.

I know this one works particularly well, so let me set the scene by way of background.

My dear friend Kevin O'Brien (gun real estate agent) is a mad keen Collingwood AFL Football Club member, and I barrack for Carlton, and we know every Carlton supporter hates Collingwood and vice versa. There is history of genuine and long-standing rivalry between the two AFL clubs and its supporters and long may it continue.

So, at one of our quarterly business review lunches, where we share our goals and hold each other to account for the achievement of them, Kevin set me a goal and major challenge *for the number of clients enrolled into my 12-month private client program by the end of the 2019 calendar year. The goals was to reach xxx number of clients registered and ready to go for 2020.* (This goal clearly meets the SMART goals framework we've just covered.)

Imagine this... if I failed to achieve my goal set with Kevin, that as a Carlton supporter I would be wearing my Carlton football jumper while standing in a queue at the Collingwood ground to buy a $200 membership ticket. Wow, I would indeed be subject to embarrassment by those opposition supporters, explaining to everyone my failed goal set with Kevin.

Naturally, and proudly, I achieved my goal and made the exact number set, by the due date. Mission accomplished; my mate Kevin feels pretty happy with himself – even though he and Collingwood missed my membership income, Kevin knew that I achieved my goal and we both had a great time, plenty of laughs and healthy banter in the build-up, with constant reminders of the consequences for failure at stake. All of this really spurred me onto great heights and wonderful success. Why not try this with a good friend? Thanks Kevin ... when's our next lunch?

And finally, you should not keep your progress to yourself. Please share it with others as it is no secret that others will want to support, advise, celebrate and counsel you if they can. This is the power of accountability, and there are plenty more examples if you delve deeper into this book.

Let me introduce you to Ned Coten

Ned is a high-level marketing and strategy consultant, also a former professional basketballer in the NBL who has now transitioned from the basketball court to the boardroom.

Ned now holds the position of Chairman of Basketball Australia, the sport's governing body. Ned still loves to roll up his sleeves as a successful entrepreneur, who also manages several other businesses in Aged Care, Self-Storage and Marketing and Business Consulting.

Ned's full bio appears below.

Bonus video

Watch, the video recording of my full interview with Ned conducted over Zoom, due to COVID restrictions and stage-4 isolation at the time of recording, on my website. Please visit: www.tickthoseboxes.com.au/TheAccountabilityAdvantage

Ned has kindly produced for our readers and viewers a slide deck (pdfs) to explain to us in more detail exactly how he and his team manages his time. Watch this as it gives an overview of the system he runs in his business, to enable him to juggle all of those balls in the air at once. Keeping them airborne, so he never misses a beat. Thanks a million, Ned. What a real treat.

Here's my discussion with Ned.

DARREN: Welcome Ned Coten, what does accountability mean to you?

NED COTEN: Thanks, Darren. It's great to sit with you and chat about it. The funny thing is as you're going through that, it makes you reflect on the things that really are important. I think to me accountability means setting an objective and making sure that you actually – and everyone is different in the way they do this – but being able to look in the mirror in the morning and say, 'I've done what I set out to do.'

And then at the end of the day going, 'Did I achieve that, or not?'

I've got a little deck here; I might take you through the slides. But one of the things I do is on my screen I keep a little note about accountability.

I think it's all up to you. At the end of the day, people who achieve anything have to be accountable to yourself.

It doesn't matter what else is happening, if you can't be accountable, if you think that someone else would say you probably haven't achieved what you should have done, and you have to be able to look at yourself in the eye and go, 'Okay, I need to lift my game.'

DARREN: You've got me interested there. What's on your screen that you've written about accountability? What does it say? Or what would a typical entry each day or week say to you?

NED COTEN: I talk about the philosophy of: understanding yourself; deciding what you want; making plans to get there; then having systems and processes to do that; and then making it fun, of course.

I say creating excitement. A lot of people say they want to be happy in life, I say you want to be excited in life. Because if you're excited, you're happy. And you can do something about being excited, but it's very hard to do something about being happy.

DARREN: I feel that entrepreneurs in the country now don't understand the true meaning of accountability. And they don't know the benefit of someone holding them to account. And not holding them to account because they've done something wrong, it's about making sure they stay on track, they stay focused. The relationship you have with Sarah, your amazing assistant, she holds you to account, you hold her to account, you work together to achieve a common goal. Entrepreneurs of today don't have that. What do you think that lack of accountability brings to individuals?

NED COTEN: That's a difficult question to think about. To me, again it might a cliché, but it's about pride. I genuinely don't really care what others think of me. I've learned to do that. But I do care what I think of myself. And I think inherently most people know that if they are really doing what they should be doing, what they are capable of doing, that they are doing a good thing for the world as a result. I think there's an incredible amount of people doing really amazing things in the world. I think that often it's because people just don't think they can, sometimes.

I believe that if it was absolutely the right thing to do, you just have to keep on going. You just have to drive until either you get to the finish line and you fall off the cliff, or you achieve what you wanted.

To me, again that simplicity about having less things – I'm certainly not perfect at it – but it's about having less things and identifying what the critical things are and just going and going and going until you can't go any further.

The Ned Coten story

Ned Coten is the CEO of EngageRM, a sports technology and CRM scaleup with a widespread client base across Australia and the US. He is the President of Basketball Australia and sits on the Competitions Commission of basketball's world body, FIBA. Ned Chairs the Advisory Board for The Contenders, one of Australia's leading brand strategy agencies, and owns and operates two successful self-storage businesses. He has investments in Aged Care, Property and Technology, while continuing as an active mentor for aspiring business leaders.

Ned has extensive experience in leadership, sports management, consumer branding, sales and marketing. He is a former CEO of a number of Australia's leading sports organisations and has operated multiple businesses as a CEO, Investor, Board Chair or Director over the past 30 years. Ned holds an MBA from the University of NSW and has written a book on branding and marketing for sport.

While attending the Australian Institute of Sport, Ned represented Australia at the 1983 World Junior Basketball Championships in Spain. He had a brief career in the National Basketball League and co-founded the Goldfields Giants in WA's State Basketball League. He holds relationships across sport and business within Australia and globally, and remains a passionate and committed volunteer, with continuous service throughout his life.

Ned has been happily married to Hilary since 1994 and has two adult sons. He resides in Melbourne, Australia.

> **'For most people, blaming others is a subconscious mechanism for avoiding accountability. In reality, the only thing in your way is YOU.'**
> *Steve Maraboli*

Chapter 2

Decide it's important that you do

Moves you to 25% – if you consciously decide you will do it.

25%

The Road to Accountability

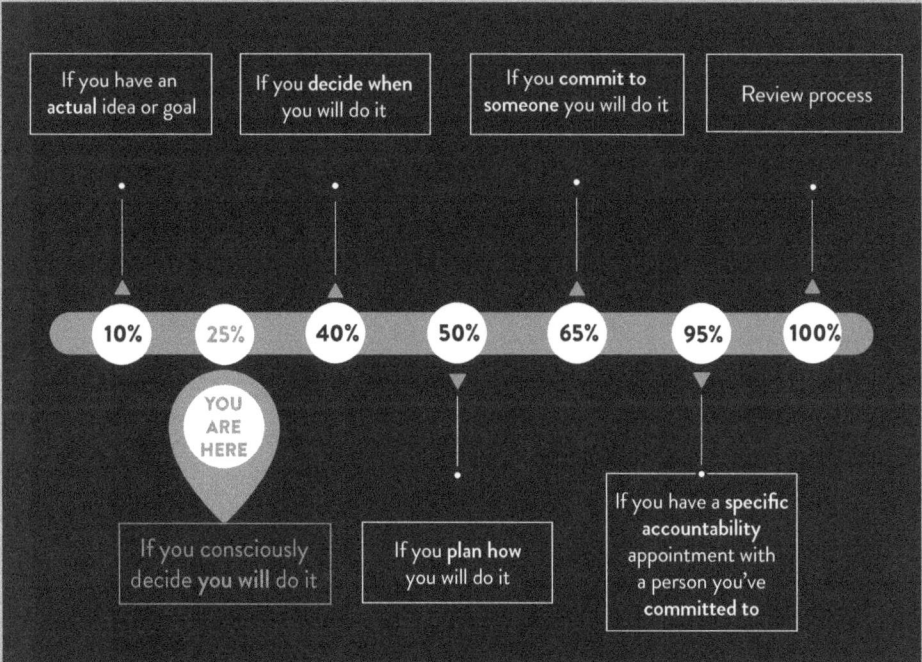

If you have an **actual** idea or goal

If you **decide when** you will do it

If you **commit to someone** you will do it

Review process

10% | 25% | 40% | 50% | 65% | 95% | 100%

YOU ARE HERE

If you consciously decide **you will do it**

If you **plan how** you will do it

If you have a **specific accountability** appointment with a person you've **committed to**

Based on the 2010 study conducted by the American Society of Training and Development (ASTD).

39

Accountability within your organisation

As we move through our timeline towards our aim of you achieving your goals with 95% probability, you can fulfill your commitments, promises, and agreements you have made to others, and especially to yourself, but first you must consciously decide you will actually do so.

Accountability in the workplace fuels successful organisations, but it can be problematic to implement if you are not seriously committed and therefore not consciously deciding that you will do it.

To consciously decide that you will do it requires you to trust your gut, your head, your heart and thereby your decision. You'll become super clear on your goal and set a North Star for everything else to fall in place behind.

> **'What you do, tells me everything about you.'**
> *Jerry Fernandez*

Accountability by name alone cannot be a hot-air balloon promise that you know is not actually being implemented. To achieve your strategy, you will need a commitment at the highest level from the people within the organisation to take responsibility for implementation.

What is so frustrating is organisations that spend a lot of time defining jobs, roles and goals in the belief that this alone will lead to better performance from its people, who will know exactly what they need to do to achieve their goals, and they understand the rewards for achievement and consequences for failure. But in reality, accountability is confusing, because rewards are misused, the consequences are diluted or never occur, which is like making a threat which you know you cannot keep, meaning that people do not understand the connection between results and recognition.

So why is accountability within your organisation being confused? According to a study by Partners in Leadership, the 'Workplace Accountability Study', a staggering 82% of respondents said they 'have no way of holding others accountable successfully'. In contrast, 91% of respondents put accountability at the forefront of their company's development needs.

Genuine accountability requires fresh honesty, which understands things can improve, and humility, which moderates action. Accountability is therefore necessary, hard to achieve, but achievable.

There is NO point in an organisation going down this path of creating a new strategic direction if your leadership is not 100% committed and the entire management team is not in agreement. If you are not all excited enough to break down the walls to achieve the outcomes identified, then you are NOT ALL IN. Hardly the positive attitude required to achieve, because no one gets what they want in life without being in a position to think about what it is to decide and agree. Then together, as one you will make a focused commitment that you want and need to take action to fix a problem, to actually achieve.

Even if it turns out that it is not the BEST choice, there is no point in getting upset about a decision that already has been reached. The train has already left the station.

The best thing you can do is learn from your mistakes for next time. Believe that you will make a better choice next time, and move on. This will help you to have more confidence in yourself and your decision-making skills.

Confident decision-making

Confident decision-making is paramount in both business and private life. As humans, we make thousands of decisions each and every day. Most decisions are simple, but others will potentially be more complicated or complex. Our more complicated and complex decisions, both in business and in your private life, can affect time, finances, feelings and relationships. The more complex decisions likely require overcoming anxiety and nervousness to execute them.

Let's discuss what 'confident decision-making' is, why it matters to your goal setting, and how you can cultivate a confident decision-making process in which you can achieve your desired goal, fulfill that task, or meet the commitment you have made to yourself and to others.

With our framework on our road to accountability nicely laid out in front of us, and easily navigable as we work towards that magical 95% probability, along our travels we are going to have to make decisions in which you will need to be confident with your decision-making. This is crucial, otherwise you will simply never get going if hesitation and procrastination reign.

'Confident decision-making' is making decisions in a manner that removes the stress and associated anxiety from those decisions, while still holding oneself responsible for actions which are true and authentic to oneself. Confident decision-making starts with the typical decision-making steps used in business.

These standard steps are:

1   Clarifying the decision.

2   Gathering data and supporting information.

3   Considering your options.

4   Reviewing and balancing evidence.

5   Listing alternative ways.

6   Time to act.

7   Time to review the decisions made.

Decision-making in all management and leadership positions can still be rather overwhelming – you can feel overwhelmed by the overwhelm.

I often find it useful to evaluate both the positive and negative emotions and feelings that emotionally engulf your process; this often helps to identify ways to improve for next time.

Listed below are some helpful tips for developing positive and confident decisions in your organisation:

- ☑ Let's not assume.

- ☑ Do not judge others.

- ☑ Seek alternative ways.

- ☑ Objectivity is important.

- ☑ Remove all attachment.

- ☑ Institution and gut feel should never be underestimated.

- ☑ Stand up and take responsibility.

- ☑ Review your decisions.

Let's have a look at each of these.

Let's not assume

Do not assume. You often make an ASS out of U and ME. It's really important to seek clarity and establish facts. Gain a solid understanding of the issues at hand in order to deal with the facts at hand.

Do not judge others

Bear in mind that your bias may not be the whole story. Trusting decision-making requires a new perspective to maintain clarity and identify all decisions as valid until you eliminate options later in your decision-making process.

Maybe write down your potential biases so you know them. This way you are aware of them and can avoid them as much as possible.

Seek alternative ways

Sometimes the options you are given do not work for the decision you have to make. Try to use your creativity and competence to create effective alternatives.

As an example, you can develop brainstorming opportunities or come up with ideas that work better and weigh the pros and cons of both.

Objectivity is important

Before making a decision, it is advantageous to know all the facts to remain objective. Normally there are many interrelated factors at play that are influenced by the weight of your decisions. You probably want to prepare for the consequences of your decisions.

To give an example, you can share your ideas with others because they can discover potential impacts you have not thought of yet.

Remove all attachment

Be aware of the possibilities, but don't cling to them. There seem to be too many unknowns in life and management. The path of confident decision-making should be the focus, not the outcome. Results are still important but should not be compulsive.

To give an example, if you have developed effective methods for rewarding your team, do you collect evidence of what it likes but is not obsessed with, what happens or what it says when it doesn't like the rewards?

Intuition and gut feel should never be underestimated

Facts and figures are important for the decision-making process. But the unique way you process and evaluate information probably puts you in your position. Normally you know the answer because there is a signal that your body gives you every day in terms of decisions.

If you have difficulty connecting with your intuition, you could do something that can reconnect you. For some people running, dancing, walking, swimming, yoga or meditation can be the answer.

Stand up and take responsibility

No matter what decision you make, you should perform it yourself and be responsible for the final decision. This is evidence of your confidence in the decisions you make when you do not blame anyone for the consequences. When things go wrong, most undertakings can be repaired and reassessed, so it is usually unnecessary to be ashamed of the result.

Own your decisions by making others aware of your choices, as long as it is appropriate for the situation.

Review your decisions

☑ Look back on past decisions and evaluate them. This is important to improve your decision-making techniques and gather information about what worked and what didn't.

Ensure that your final decision is as good as any input, research and facts you have gathered.

I hear you ask why it is so important to make decisions on the basis of trust. An important question. Here are my thoughts.

Self-confident decisions for leadership goals are crucial for the functioning of you and your employees in the workplace. If you make firm and confident decisions, your confidence will be strengthened, you will be much more positive in your movements and you will probably be able to eliminate unpleasant feelings in different areas of your work and private life.

Here are some reasons confident decision-making is important:

☑ You have already taken steps to achieve your goals to a considerable extent by clearly identifying what is happening to them within the framework of the SMART goals framework.

☑ Taking the first step was always the hardest part of the challenge. Now that you have made up your mind, you have a goal; you must do something about it, hence the time for decision.

☑ The company with the most famous catchphrase in the world is Nike: 'Just do it'. In your case, you now need to consciously decide you are going to go after your goal, which has become much clearer now you've got it in the SMART goal format for simplicity.

So, let's take you through step by step of how to TRUST yourself to decide to go after your goals consciously.

Trusting your gut

How do you do things?

If you want to trust your gut feeling, you need to know what it tells you. You have to know what a gut feeling is: language only plays a role in communicating with people. In fact, it is the brain that works diligently to collect tiny micro signals that communicate what a human foresees.

This explains how people often have a 'gut feeling' or intuition about a person or situation even if they cannot logically determine why.

Some executives pride themselves on having strong intuition – sharpened by years of experience – that guides their decisions. Others rely ambitiously on their intuition for important decisions, because they fear their gut instinct is inherently biased or emotional. The latter group undoubtedly responds to the often-repeated advice that we should test our intuitions on the basis of formal data and analysis.

What happens when you make a decision?

The role of memory in decision making – and sometimes in making bad decisions – is really important to researchers, economists, and psychologists who have focused on trying to figure out how we process and complete decisions.

Different areas seem to take different approaches to analysing decision making. Economists seem to focus more on what we should ideally do to make the right choice or decision, whereas psychologists focus more on what decisions we actually make. Some of us stick to what we are used to and/or what gives us a sense of security.

Other people are taking a risk when they make a decision and decide for the unknown, the difficult and the innovative. Indeed, risk strongly influences our decisions, which can be divided into risky and risk-free. If there is logically more risk involved, it is more likely to make a bad decision. It is more or less risky to make a bet compared to the risk-free choice between pasta or pizza. Neither, if you rely on a calorie-based diet.

Benefit can also influence our decisions – and it is determined by the balance between risk and benefit – although this balance can be perceived differently at the time of decision due to influencing factors such as our affective/emotional state and time stress. A number of our decisions are based on probability judgements about possible outcomes and when perceived probabilities prevail over objective probabilities. If that is the case, that is a bad decision.

Perceived probabilities, our understanding of the possible outcomes of a decision, just like those in the road to accountability can be influenced by current events and encounters, emotional states and other factors can lead to more mistakes and wrong decisions, hence the need for someone to hold you to account and keep a steady course. Remember, you are responsible for things and accountable to people.

Trusting your head

In addition to the mere decision with the belly, you must also consider with the head. Which LOGICAL decision makes sense?

The problem many of us face is there is often more than one way to do something. It can sometimes be overwhelming, leading to inaction, because we end up doing nothing, because it's too complex to choose.

A tried-and-tested technique is the 'pros and cons list'.

However, it is a conventional technique, which often does not provide the required results. Solely because there appear more pros than cons do not necessarily mean you have to agree with the pro option. A particular choice on this list may have a greater weighting and this method is therefore not always correct.

Trusting your heart

After all, it is time to understand what your heart tells you: the intention behind the decisions. Conscious decision-making has to come from the heart. Otherwise, it is ultimately a futile pursuit of your goals.

Trust in one's heart is often met with suspicion because it is a philosophical concept.

However, it is based on:

☑ **Your values of making decisions** that satisfy you and are in line with what you consider important will undoubtedly lead to more decision-making. This is aligned with your WHY and purpose.

☑ **Time is one of the determining factors for how you think,** how much time you spend doing something. Make a calculation before you decide whether it is worth investing time, money or energy. 'Reward for effort' is my go-to for deciding which way to go. I often ask myself the question: is the reward for all this effort a fair compensation for my time needed to make it happen? Do the sums: time vs $$$.

☑ **Meditating and mindfulness** – one of the most profound ways to engage with matters of the heart is to sit down and meditate and practise the art of mindfulness. Sometimes the reactions of the heart can be blocked by 'noise'. Meditation removes the sound and allows you to synchronise with your heart.

Trusting your decision

Now that you have brought your gut feeling, your heart and your mind together, it is important that you do not ignore any of them when making a decision. It is a question of harmonising these various elements, which you must account for.

A misalignment between the gut, heart, and mind leads to **cognitive dissonance** – a psychological term for the state that arises because of a contradiction between your beliefs – which makes you feel torn between two outcomes.

DO NOT suppress any of the three aspects we are talking about. It only leads to discomfort and discontent. Here is a quick exercise:

Apart from the decision-making process and understanding, if you simply **do not have a sufficient reason** to achieve your goal, it may not happen. If you do not have a BIG enough reason to get the job or the project done, there is NO real motivation to get your goal achieved.

Normally you would move on to the next project and leave this one largely unfinished, as this project does not have sufficient reason for you to focus on completing and achieving your goal:

☑ You need to reconnect with this project and understand WHY you must complete it.

☑ Understand the importance of the role you play and how your effort impacts others. This will remind you of the responsibility you have to play your part and not let others down.

I can find lots of procrastination techniques to keep me from reaching the finish line. That's when I take a few minutes to visualise what it means to be finished with the project – then I push hard to power through and get it done.

Guess what? There appear to be millions of people on this planet who are willing to get up every morning, get dressed, and drag themselves to work so that someone else can tell them what to do. It takes a real leader to make a decision. They set the direction and are ultimately prepared to bear the burden of responsibility for success or failure on their shoulders. In General Norman Schwarzkopf's autobiography, *It Doesn't Take a Hero*, he shares 14 rules for leadership. Rule 13 says, 'When placed in command, take charge'. Plain and simple.

Making a decision is the only way forward. Yes, even incorrect decisions are better that no decisions. A person who makes a thousand wrong decisions is better off than one who makes no decisions at all.

Why? Because a person who has acquired a thousand wrong decisions has excluded a thousand things that do not work, and has therefore made progress. They are much better prepared to move forward towards success than the person who is in day four of watching PowerPoint presentations on Plan A vs Plan B.

Nobody is proposing you skip due diligence. However, as I have already outlined, you must learn how to trust your gut feeling, trust your head, trust your heart and trust your decision, so that you can move forward.

Let me introduce you to Bruce Levy

I have recorded a Zoom session with Bruce, who is a former senior executive and leader in the health industry. Bruce retired only six weeks ago at the time of this interview.

Bruce is generous with his time; after all, I'm getting him out of his retirement for an hour or so to share his thoughts about working in giant organisations. Specifically, we talk about how teams make decisions, and how accountability and responsibility are key to achieving your desired outcomes. It's nice to get a perspective on exactly how organisations roll at the BIG end of town.

Bruce has had a wonderful career in senior management with leading players in health insurance, law and other industries, in such roles as the former CEO of Medibank Private Health Insurance and he was General Manager for The Alfred Hospital in Melbourne for some time, one of the largest hospitals and emergency facilities in the southern hemisphere.

Bruce's full bio appears below.

Bonus video

Watch the entire video recording of my full interview with Bruce conducted over Zoom, due to COVID restrictions and stage-4 isolation at the time of recording. It is available for viewing from my website. Please visit: www.tickthoseboxes.com.au/TheAccountabilityAdvantage

Here's my discussion with Bruce.

DARREN: Bruce, I want to focus today's conversation on accountability. What does accountability mean to you?

BRUCE LEVY: I suppose accountability means to me understanding what's important and being held to deliver or meet that. What's important can be direct or indirect, it can be spoken or unspoken, it could be soft in the sense of establishing an environment like a culture or a set of values, it could be hard in the sense of delivering a profit or whatever it may be.

But you've got to determine within that what's important, and then you've got to determine how you're going to be measured on making sure you meet what's important.

DARREN: You're talking about prioritising what is more important than something else?

BRUCE LEVY: Sometimes it's prioritising, sometimes it's just being aware in everything you do sitting in the background of what's important. For example, I believe, and my experience through the corporate world has shown, that culture and values are just as important as the hard targets of budgets and cash flows and the lot. Doesn't mean I necessarily prioritise culture and values over that, it just means I've got to create the environment for culture and values to enable me to be successful on the hard aspects (the KPIs and the KIAs – whatever people call them nowadays). Me personally, I know that if I keep the values and cultural aspects always close to my mind, then I spend more time running around and trying to deliver on the KPIs that I might be given.

So, it's just getting that balance right. If you prioritise too hard, then you get lost in that quandary of what's urgent versus what's important.

DARREN: How you determine what is important versus what's urgent?

BRUCE LEVY: The best way is having a strong connection and dependable access to those to whom you're accountable. Whether I'm a CEO accountable to a board or a senior management accountable to a managing director, I've got to take the time to make sure I get clarity as to what's important. Because if that person comes along and says to me, 'Bruce, I want you to do x tomorrow,' and that's just a knee-jerk because someone's giving them a task, that then becomes urgent. But if that clashes with what's important because I'm working on something that goes to my core accountability, then I've got to call that out. I've got to say: I can do that, it might mean it's going to take a week of my time (or whatever it might be), so I've got to be absolutely clear. To do that I've got to: A; have a good rapport with the individual or the group of individuals, and B; I've got to have the strength to ask if I think there's a conflict or insufficient clarity. Because there will always be a clash of time, a clash of resources, never enough time or resources to do everything. So, it's up to me to seek clarity, and part of that is active listening as well as open questions to make sure I extract exactly what they want.

The Bruce Levy story

After 40 years in the corporate world, Bruce has now officially retired from all corporate and executive work.

Using the disruption caused by COVID-19, Bruce decided to step down from his last role that has seen him working for four years in Shanghai as a FIFO worker, on behalf of Luye Medical Pte.

And reflecting on his career, who could have asked for a better 'swansong' role – managing the complex relationship between the Chinese-based Luye Medical and the US-based Cleveland

Clinic Foundation, concerning the development of a campus of private hospital facilities in downtown Shanghai.

After his 'first retirement' when he stepped down from his CEO role at Medibank Private in 2013 that led to him and his wife moving interstate from Melbourne to Bellingen on the mid north coast of NSW, initially his time was split between living in and operating their fantastic B&B, the Lilly Pilly Country House, coupled with local community work in the Bellingen Shire and a variety of NED (Non-Executive Director) and advisory roles across the health and insurance sectors.

Eventually selling Lilly Pilly, and while doing some executive leadership work for Healthe Care Australia, following their acquisition by the Chinese Luye Medical Group, and before Bruce knew it he was busy working with a small team from HCA bringing the Australian private health care knowledge and expertise into the rapidly growing China private hospital market.

This role then grew into establishing a long-term collaboration agreement with the Cleveland Clinic, one of the US's top hospital groups, and then managing that contract between the Chinese and US teams, an interesting time to be doing this.

Prior to this, from 2010 to 2011 Bruce was the Non-Executive Director of Ambulance Victoria and The General Manager of Alfred Heath from 1995 to 2002, establishing The Alfred Hospital as one of Australia's busiest emergency and Trauma Centres. Incorporating the state's largest Intensive Care Unit, and home to multiple statewide services with Victoria's only heart and lung transplant service, the Victorian Adults Burn Service and the Victorian Melanoma Service. Patients come to The Alfred for specialty services like comprehensive cancer care, respiratory medicine, cardiology and cardiovascular services, and in-patient and community psychiatry care.

Since international travel is unlikely in the foreseeable future, Bruce decided it was time to retire from all board work and refocus on his work with his local community, to undertake some property development, and spend as much time as possible with Jeannette, his family and friends and on his beloved longboard at his favourite spot in Arrawarra Headland, NSW.

'Action springs not from thought, but from a readiness for responsibility.'
Dietrich Bonhoeffer

Chapter 3

Set priorities

Moves you to 40% – if you decide when you will do it.

40%

The Road to Accountability

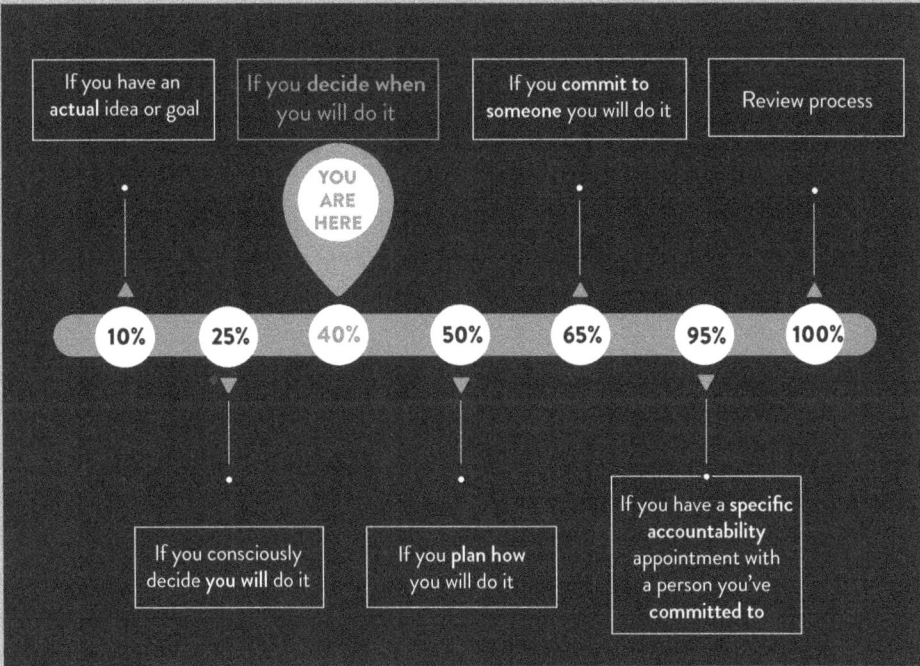

If you have an **actual** idea or goal

If you decide when you will do it

If you **commit to someone** you will do it

Review process

YOU ARE HERE

10% · 25% · 40% · 50% · 65% · 95% · 100%

If you consciously decide **you will** do it

If you **plan how** you will do it

If you have a **specific accountability** appointment with a person you've **committed to**

Based on the 2010 study conducted by the American Society of Training and Development (ASTD).

W̲e are moving on down the road to accountability, and I hear you say, 'are we there yet?' just like the kids on a long journey. Not yet, but we are nearly halfway at 40% probability, which awaits you at the completion of this chapter. You are well on your way to getting your to-do list 'to-done'.

You're now at the point where you have set clear goals, and consciously thought them through, being able to make confident decisions along the way. To ensure we don't get ahead of ourselves, there is a potential stumbling block along our journey, and that is our ability to prioritise goals.

We are humans, and we are all unique in terms of our emotions, egos, personalities and values, so setting priorities for you is not usually the same as the priorities I will set for myself. After talking with many clients and their teams over a number of years, this is a genuine problem because we quite often try to impart our own individual priorities onto someone else. Therefore, understanding that what's important to me is NOT always important to someone else. This means that my priorities are not your priorities, and vice versa.

In this chapter, you'll understand how to set your priorities on our road to accountability, and we'll cover:

☑ Setting your priorities

    ✓ Let's play dominoes and eat an elephant

    ✓ The Eisenhower Matrix

☑ Putting your 'to-do list' in ONE place

☑ Darren's 5D's

During my interview with Rob Nankervis, a business coach and corporate advisor in chapter 4, Rob shares with us that setting priorities is a lot like playing with a set of dominoes ...

Rob says, 'Remember, those small rectangular black tiles that we often played with as kids and as adults? Now imagine setting them up end on end, to form a long, long line. Just imagine for the moment that each of those dominoes are individual tasks, projects and/or goals which you want to complete, but you simply don't know where to start.'

Rob beautifully describes the need to pick the very first domino – that is, task, project or goal – which is going to represent the biggest single difference to you or your organisation. Focus on that domino, and individually flick that domino over; no strength is required, just an ever so slight touch which triggers ALL of the other dominoes to fall ...

Let's think of that domino you touched as a task, project or goal – this is the one you choose to begin with. It is this analogy which best describes what you're looking do to when you set your priorities. Find the single domino (task, project or goal) which has the maximum effect, and do that one first.

Rob's domino theory is closely aligned with that of investment guru and legend Warren Buffett and his famous 5/25 rule. Warren in his wisdom said this about setting your priorities:

☑   Write down the 25 goals you want to achieve.

☑   Circle the top 5 goals.

☑   Never think about the other 20 goals again.

Simple in its thinking and makes total sense. The 20 remaining goals will take your focus away from the top 5, which now need to be your top priority.

Let's move from dominoes to elephants. Desmond Tutu is an iconic South African cleric recognised for his amazing work as an anti-apartheid and human rights activist. Desmond once astutely said that 'there is only one way to eat an elephant – one bite at a time'. His meaning relates directly to the fact that everything appears to be so overwhelming, the elephant is too large in its physical size that the only way to get through the elephant's obvious volume is to break it down into smaller bite-sized chunks, then grapple with these a little bit at a time. This not only makes total sense, but it's a really clever and effective process for removing the overwhelm, procrastination and anxiety associated with not being able to set priorities and begin working towards your goal or task.

The Eisenhower Matrix

Let's take a look at the popular 'Eisenhower Matrix' for identifying and setting your priorities, which is used heavily by C-suite executives, business owners and entrepreneurs all over the world. Much of my research on the Eisenhower Matrix was acquired from www.Eisenhower.me

Dwight Eisenhower was the 34th President of the United States during the years 1953 to 1961. Eisenhower had been a Five-Star General from the United States military and served as supreme commander of the Allied Forces in Europe during World War II.

Eisenhower developed a great method to increase his productiveness, which worked very successfully for him in the years before his passing. Today, his unique approaches to productiveness have been studied and used productively by high-achieving specialists, athletes, professionals, musicians and so forth.

His easiest strategy – known as 'the Eisenhower Matrix' – is an easy, highly effective method which helps to better prioritise your endeavours by differentiating between that which is pressing and important.

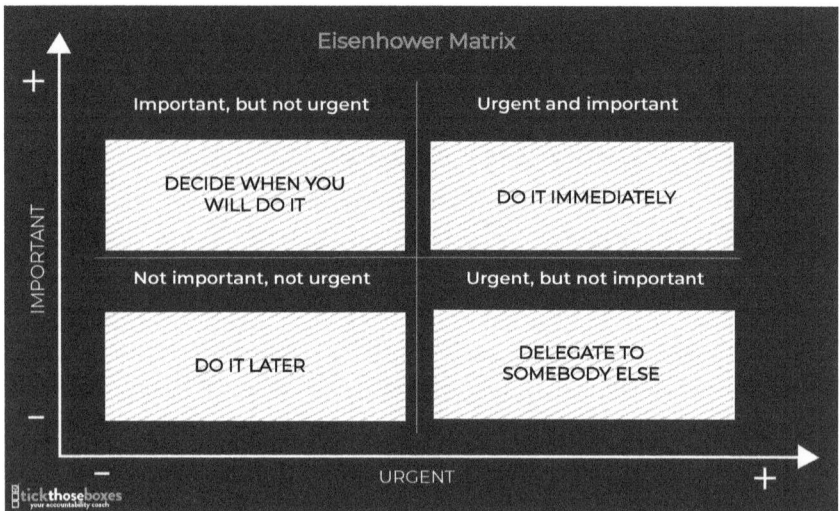

Source: www.eisenhower.me

Initially popularised in the book *The 7 Habits of Highly Successful People* by Stephen Covey, The Eisenhower Matrix, also referred to as the Urgent–Important Matrix, includes four well-considered quadrants which assist you to decide on and prioritise activities with urgency and value, as shown on the previous page.

The four quadrants of the Eisenhower Matrix are as follows:

1   Urgent and important (activities to do instantly).

2   Important, but not urgent (actions to program afterwards).

3   Urgent, however perhaps not important (actions to assign to someone else).

4   Neither urgent nor important (actions to expel).

Eisenhower had to make tough decisions continuously, about which of the many tasks he should focus on each day. This finally led him to invent the Eisenhower Matrix, which today helps us prioritise by urgency and importance.

'The maximum intensity conclusions are hardly ever probably the main ones.'
Dwight Eisenhower

How to use the Eisenhower matrix

This visual method of time management, also called Urgent–Important Matrix, divides tasks into four quadrants to prioritise the order of completion. The fields are marked one to four and each has a specific action point: Do, Decide, Delegate or Delete.

☑   **Do:** Urgent and important (tasks to be done immediately).

☑   **Decide:** Important but not urgent (tasks you should prioritise and plan, to avoid a last-minute rush).

☑   **Delegate:** Urgent but not important (urgent but menial tasks, like meetings that get in the way of the important ones).

☑   **Delete:** Not urgent and not important (tasks which only serve to waste time and which can be deleted from the to-do list).

Traffic Light Method: My take on the popular method

The 'Traffic Light' method, also known as the 'Green, Amber (or Yellow), Red' (GAR) status system, is a popular tool for setting priorities and monitoring progress in project management and business strategy. It's a simple, visual method of indicating the status of various tasks or objectives, similar to how traffic lights control traffic flow.

Here's my take on this, with my modified explanations of each status, to better suit my needs. It comes with age; I like to call that my 'grey-haired wisdom' shining through.

1. Green (GO)

A 'green' status in this method indicates that a task or project requires your immediate attention; think GO, GO, GO. It's a sign that something needs to be done *right now* – we want maximum acceleration here. A green status could be defined by missed deadlines, exceeded budgets, or underachievement of key performance indicators (KPIs). The green status encourages team members and management to get to work; do not delegate this; you must do this task yourself, and do it now with a sense of urgency.

Personally, I like to prioritise potential green tasks by determining whether or not they are green by answering yes to two simple questions. They are:

☑ Does this task have to be completed within the next seven days? *To increase your sense of urgency here, insert your own number of days (or hours) depending on what's required.*

☑ Must I complete this task and not delegate it to others?

It's simple to determine whether this task is green or not, thereby removing all emotions and uncertainty.

Once you have a list of all the green classifications, you must allocate the necessary time in your schedule/diary to complete each task in full, within the next seven days, or whatever time you set as your deadline – it could theoretically be 24 to 48 hours.

If you don't have time, you'll have to sacrifice something to make this work. It is pointless to have an urgent task with no time to complete it; something must give. Otherwise, you will be unable to complete the task.

Now that it's locked in and loaded, all you have to do is stick to your schedule/diary and complete the task within the time limit.

2. Amber/Yellow (CAUTION)

An 'amber' or 'yellow' status serves as a reminder that the task can be completed by someone else (yes, you can delegate) or by you, but only after you have completed the green tasks. That means those tasks may only be completed after the green day/ hour deadline, or as soon as someone else you delegate it to can. It's not an emergency.

3. Red (STOP)

A 'red' status indicates that you should not be performing this task yourself. There is danger, danger, and more danger. It usually means that the project or task is on track, within the defined parameters such as time and budget, and is progressing well towards the goals, but you should devote more time to other things. It is a red task that you must not complete on your own, so find someone else to do it for you. Your time should be spent on other activities. For you, red represents danger; it is a warning sign, a big flashing light not to be distracted or drawn into something you do not need to be doing.

Who should you delegate it to? Good question, perhaps a team member who wants to step up and take on more responsibility, maybe a team member who has interests in this specific area or a similar field, or perhaps hand it over to someone who is looking for more things to do or more challenges, because they are ahead of the game or even one of the lucky ones who have additional time on their side.

Some suggestions, to help you on your way

Make an educated guess about how long it will take you to complete each task and write it next to your tasks.

If you've previously completed this task, this will be simple; if not, make your best guess. You can get an exact number by adjusting your times for the next To-Do List after the previous one is completed. Now that you're paying more attention to the timings of your tasks, you'll quickly get an idea of how much time it takes to actually complete a task. You will be surprised at what you find.

The key to performing this exercise well and on a regular basis, say once a week, is to train a team member to perform the 'classification process' for you. This means the sorting and sifting of your tasks into Green, Amber, and Red categories is critical. Do this every week, set a meeting with your classification person, and you'll soon see your productivity will skyrocket.

Remember, here's what my modified colours represent:

Green (Go, go, go – action is needed)

☑ You must do it (you cannot delegate)

☑ You must do it within (?) days

☑ Add this task to your schedule/diary time immediately

Amber

☑ Someone else can do (please delegate)

☑ You can do it, but only after all the greens are done. If so, add this task to your schedule/diary time immediately

Red (Danger, ganger, danger, it will distract you)

☑ You should not be doing this task

☑ Yes, you must delegate to others
Consider delegation to:
– someone wanting to step-up
– find someone with interest in this area
– someone who has available time.

Urgent vs important

Urgent responsibilities encompass time-sensitive responsibilities. These are activities that require immediate attention and include telephone calls, meetings and immediate crises. Important questions are, however, of the utmost importance for growth and often of an evolutionary nature. They contribute to the picture and are often pushed aside when urgent tasks are to be done.

As you can imagine, the problem is that when important tasks fade into the background, the business stagnates and remains immobile or proceeds more slowly than you would like. This is particularly true for the important but non-urgent tasks in the second quadrant, which we often overlook, while tasks in the first and third quadrants and often even in the fourth quadrant have priority.

The distinction between 'urgent' and 'important' helps you to share your thoughts and make decisions. In this way, the Eisenhower Matrix offers blameless permission to focus on tasks that are important for the first two quadrants and eliminate anything that does not contribute positively to your role.

The distinction between 'urgent' and 'important' helps you to share your thoughts and make decisions.

Deciding what's important

It is, of course, a never-ending task to determine where everything should fit into the Eisenhower matrix, especially when it comes to deciding what is important.

The best place to start is to create a to-do list to help you visualise your tasks. After all, understanding the extent of your obligations when they are written on paper is easier than running around like you have flies in your head.

The next step is to look at the list and ask yourself two questions: would the impact be significant if this task were not fulfilled, and can you delegate this task? Sometimes the urgent tasks require us to be so blind that we consider them more important than they are. If you can remove a task from your to-do list without compromising business, do so. If it is possible to hand over the task to a colleague, this may not be so important for you personally.

Once you have a good idea of what an important task is, you can start to divide the tasks by urgency. I hope that this step will be more important than the previous one. If it needs to be completed today or in the next couple of days, then it's urgent. If you can put it off until later, then it's probably not so urgent.

After you set up your matrix, your next task is to get moving! You are likely to find that your priorities are changing, which may seem a bit daunting at first glance. But the goal of the Eisenhower Matrix is to bolster proactivity, and as time goes on, it should become easier and clearer.

Not knowing where to start

In my top seven reasons why people don't **G**et **S**h!t **D**one list, which I'll cover later in greater detail, *Not knowing where to start* features highly.

When you don't know where to start an exercise and you struggle to begin is called **procrastination**, and with this comes the likelihood that you will never actually begin unless you get outside assistance.

The first step towards starting a task or goal, even when you don't know what you're doing, is to understand that you cannot control when ideas, inspiration, and light bulb moments might come to you. Our minds are always working like a sponge, trying to absorb everything that comes.

You can save those ideas, steward them, and even tell them NO not yet, but you cannot restrain them from arriving unannounced at your doorstep just because you're taking a break:

☑ Idea gremlins show up and disrupt the soul without explanation. If you try to figure them out before it's time, it will only end in frustration.

☑ Instead, let them come. Let them dance. Let them turn over some tables. See what they have to say without demanding they have a reason.

☑ Write them down and save them for later, as there are usually fragments of gold among them which you don't want to dismiss. Keeping them for later and considering them at another time is a smart idea.

My **'Ideas Bank'** booklet is the perfect place to write your important business ideas and thoughts until you are ready to act. When you are ready, and the time is right. Perfect for those entrepreneurs who generate loads of ideas, and wish to keep them until they are ready! You are welcome to download it for free, visit: www.tickthoseboxes.com.au/free-stuff/

Keith Abraham CSP, a legendary speaker on the professional speaking circuit, did a post on social media recently that truly caught my eye. Keith wrote:

> *Procrastination is the greatest robber of self-confidence. It eats away at you and makes you feel bad about you.*
>
> *Focus is the greatest enhancer of self-confidence, so forget about starting, just focus on taking the first step.*
>
> *Remember this – 'the day you take the first step of the task you have been procrastinating about – the task that may be holding you back – is the day you beat procrastination!'*

If you have always wanted to achieve something great, you know that getting started can be a challenge. Perhaps you only have a rough idea of what you actually want, but no idea how to go about it. Or you sit down and think about everything you have to do, and you get completely intimidated and overwhelmed, numb, and feel unable to take the first step because you do not know where, or how, to establish a place to start.

This is a shared experience; everyone has experienced this at some time, yet it is a weighty reason why so many people are unable to realise their goals and dreams. They try to eat the whole elephant in a single bite. How accurate and on the money is Desmond Tutu with his explanation?

I know that we live in a world of intense distraction, which, coupled with a perceived lack of time, forces us to spend our day multitasking and overloading ourselves in an attempt to get things done. The results of our efforts are predictable, as many studies show that in business, we have some difficulty concentrating and managing time. This is supported by proven facts which we find difficult to accept. The best managers of time know exactly how to concentrate and stay focused, otherwise it is tantalising to head to the next task long before the previous one is finished and ticked off their to-do list once and for all. As a result, they try to take on more tasks or goals, and yet while these responsibilities are usually taken on for all the right reasons, they desperately try hard and end up taking on too many things at the one time. Then, they wonder why nothing gets finished – because our brains are not wired for multitasking.

If we cannot concentrate and focus, we are acting with a distinct lack of intention. What is this 'intention' you ask? Intention is best described as *'mental orientation for something,'* just like determining the preferred outcome of a goal you have identified with our implementation of the SMART goal process, which we covered earlier. The intention is to know what you want from an activity; it is at the intersection of the urge to concentrate and the action of correct and timely execution of a specific activity. You cannot concentrate without focusing your attention on a particular task or goal, and doing so with an intensity like our magnifying glass burning in the schoolyard. We only need the one thing that you approach purposefully and intensively, and that is which task or goal do you choose first? Now, setting priorities here is in line with your path of responsibility.

Do you struggle to **G**et **S**h!t **D**one because *everything* appears important? Jeez, I do – I get it … For this reason, I feel empathy for all those who want to do everything right, now that time is short and there is always so much to do. I get that. Moving in a certain direction is such a pleasant and comfortable feeling, but all that comfort changes instantly when you receive that dreaded call, read those text messages or check those emails to say that something has not gone according to plan that you need to address right now. This forces you to make a detour from your plan, which is a distraction from the intended direction. We have all received phone calls and messages that go straight into the pit of your stomach, leaving you disillusioned with the situation. They say that the squeaky cog gets the oil, which is appropriate and must be at the top of your list in this case, as customer satisfaction is the absolute key to a strong and successful company. Without satisfied clients willing to recommend you to others, I question whether you have a business or not.

Shiny object syndrome

One of the biggest struggles many of my clients face as entrepreneurs, along with C-suite executives across the nation and their teams, has been overcoming the shiny object syndrome.

Shiny object syndrome is when you digress from your road to chase something which has got your attention away from what you are doing, onto something else. You either think you should be following others in your space because that is what everyone is doing, or you spot an object shining out of the corner of your eye which captures your immediate attention, so you digress as it draws your journey in different direction. This naturally costs you valuable time; it draws your energy away and it hinders your ability to stay on course.

Here's six ways in which shiny object syndrome can reveal itself in your business:

☑ Your attention and focus being shared among too many different tasks, goals and projects at the same time, such as business strategy, product distribution, sales funnels, and commission structure for your outbound sales team.

☑ You find yourself downloading and playing with a bunch of new software and technology that doesn't need to be tested and nor do they need to be implemented right now. They will not help you complete your immediate task, project or goal.

☑ You're enrolled in several online courses at the same time, so you lose focus on the important stuff.

☑ You have an ever-growing pile of unfinished projects on your to-do list which are simply not getting done.

☑ Your to-do list is ever growing and you just cannot make any headway.

☑ Nothing is ever launched.

Shiny object syndrome causes a complete breakdown of productivity, a total lack of strategy and loss of direction, so don't be tempted. It's rather like a racehorse who wears blinkers on the track, to stay looking forward at their goal so they don't look sideways, searching for shiny objects which distract.

Are there any acceptable distractions?

Do you find your focus wavering at times? Maybe you get distracted from your goal and have a hard time getting back on track. Or maybe you're like many people that I talk to and you have a hard time defining exactly what your goals are; what it is you're working for.

Most of us get side-tracked at times. **But how you bring yourself back to where you need to be is critical.** I truly believe having the ability to maintain focus in a noisy, distracted and hyper-busy world is vital. What distractions are stopping you from tapping into your true potential or achieving all that you are capable of? Once you have identified what they are, you can begin to starve them out.

Being in business is really hard, and you have to juggle a lot of balls successfully at all times. Normally we would like to have a few hours more a day in addition to the 24-hour clock; if you find a way to do that, you will please millions of businesspeople, making them very happy! But that will be short-lived, as the vast majority of us are actually striving to work fewer hours, so that we can have time to do other things that are also important in our lives.

With a shortage of hours in your day to do everything you want, and to do it correctly, if you have said yes to too many things, don't worry, there is enough time given you probably already have a rough idea of what your priorities are. Congratulations, many of your peers do not.

Without clear priorities, it's often far too difficult to manage your time and to make progress with the achievement of your goals because you will not be able to choose what you need to do first. How will you decide on which of the dominoes to push, to have the biggest impact and effect? Which finds you in a world of overwhelm, trying to take on too many responsibilities at once.

As a result, procrastination sets in as you cannot find the place to start. With all the internal processing and mind-wrestling of what to do and when, you actually do not do anything at all because you cannot clearly decide.

The truth is, our ability to move forward and achieve our desired outcomes greatly depends on what priorities we set to begin with. Once you are clear with your priorities, you will be in a position to make better and faster decisions that will shape your life and business. It is finding the head domino, then watching with pride as they all fall from just the smallest amount of force. A breath of air as you exhale will just about do it.

Priorities are those areas in our lives that are the most meaningful and important to us. Mostly, these are activities, practices or relationships in which we want to invest real effort and time. Priorities imply that a hierarchy can be maintained for various areas of your life and work.

Instead of believing that *everything* is important, priorities help you to choose what to focus on first. When I found out my top priorities, it helped me realise that *I don't have to do everything*. If I want to say NO to someone now, it is much easier to tell them NO because this is just not one of my priorities at the moment. I don't feel guilty about saying NO, and it doesn't feel like I'm making excuses to get out of something. Knowing your life priorities will ultimately help you decide how you prioritise your day-to-day tasks.

A good long-standing client approached me and asked me about the difference between priorities and goals. She tried to stay focused in her business and achieve certain goals, but she was not sure how to clearly identify her goals and set priorities. In my opinion, goals are the overarching picture, tangible milestones that we are trying to achieve.

To give you a real-life, relatable example of what I'm talking about, let's use my writing this book as an example.

Right now, I'm writing my manuscript chapter by chapter, each one as a Microsoft Word document. Once all of the chapters are written, I'll add the foreword to be written by someone special and connected to my why and to my purpose. Next step is to add my introduction, which sets the scene, and my manuscript will be completed. Then it goes to my publisher and their process begins turning my words into a wonderfully presented, completed product that gets delivered to me in perfectly packed recycled brown boxes. I'll open the first boxes with much excitement and a little trepidation as I observe my 'child' for the very first time. Naturally, I'll celebrate my achievement. I'm putting the date in my diary as 1 February 2021, which will be my release date. This date is the culmination of everything that has been done so far; each step can be complicated, but in terms of complexity it has to be completed in a certain way, at a certain date and at a certain time, for my release date to occur.

To set and meet priorities I know there are matters which I am going say *either YES or NO* to in order for me to reach that goal on time, and meet my 1 February 2021 deadline.

To achieve this, I've broken down my list of tasks required, set my priorities –yes, I found that one domino to kick it off – and created deadlines to ensure the completion of my manuscript no later than the end of October 2020. I deconstructed the outcome, the specific goal I set, and calculated all of the steps backwards from that point in order to find the beginning. Deconstructing and working backwards like this is an absolutely wonderful exercise and so incredibly useful. It is the solid foundation we all need for getting started. If you combine my five favourite goal setting questions that brought a close to chapter 1, what are they?

☑   Where are you now?

☑   Where would you like to be?

☑   What's been stopping you?

☑   How do you want to get there?

☑   Why is it an absolute must?

Michael and Anna from Publish Central are my book publishers, and they need my manuscript before the end of October to begin their process of creating and producing my book. Upon receipt, the team at Publish Central have a few rounds on editing, rewriting, and proofreading to ensure 'Darren's English' is replaced by the 'Queen's English'; apparently my readers will be more comfortable with that. Then they mobilise their team and get into full swing. They will design the cover and the spine, typeset my pages, they will sort out the page layout for both the paperback and eBook versions, ensuing we've got all reading formats and reader preferences covered.

As my focus is set to ensuring all of my priorities for the book are completed by the due dates which are set for each item, I have a singular focus, and it's this emphasis which underpins me saying NO more often to other distractions which hold me back from meeting my deadlines and plan. Groceries, household chores, etc. are usually done first (unless I can get out of them), so I'm free to clearly focus on working through my plans and priorities with an eye on my goals, with as little outside distraction as possible.

This works for me – in fact, I know exactly what works best. I understand the how and what I need to do with my focus, with my planning and with my rituals to manage my projects.

I did meet my submission deadline.

I get that with practice and hard, self-critical analysis of the times I've failed and you will do that, hopefully fewer times than when you succeed. That's me keeping myself accountable and myself to account for the things I say I'm going to.

Now that I'm a four-time author, including this book, I bet you didn't know that? Each time I sit to write, hopefully painting very clear pictures for my readers while taking the reader on a journey of self-discovery, my goals are to take you on the road to accountability for yourself, and that it works so well that you get your team to do the same. It's the application of my framework and modules into readers' lives, both at a personal and business level, that determines whether my book achieves its goals or not. 'Taking action' is a cure for all.

My favourite days for writing are the weekends, when I've got both Saturday and Sunday to write. My writing sessions usually last four to eight hours, depending on 'how in the zone' I am.

I always make a ritual of preparing well. I know specifically what I want to achieve from each session, and set that as my goal. I know what I want my target word count to be, I know how much time I can allocate if my execution goes well. If it doesn't, I will cut my writing day short and take a break, largely to avoid the complete frustration of trying unsuccessfully to make this writing session work, but sometimes it just does not. I know when to stop, pull up stumps and try again another day when I'm fresh. This break gives me time to decompress and restructure my thoughts, and to review and fine tune my plan if need be.

Preparation is key, and this begins well before I sit down at the keyboard to actually write, so I don't ever get writer's block which you've likely seen on TV or in movies. The writer is seen in the classic Hollywood movie set; they are sitting in front of the trusty typewriter and they continually pull out paper, screw it up and throw it away in frustration, leaving a pile of unfinished pages on the floor. Get what I mean... we've all seen that on the big screen before. I see this quandary as merely poor preparation. The excuse of 'writer's block' is unhelpful and only makes matters worse. Whereas taking personal responsibility for the lack of proper planning and ineffective preparation before they sit down at the keyboard is the root problem. To me, I see **excuses, blame and finger pointing** being created subconsciously, as a means of handling the personal let-down and sense of dissatisfaction with ourselves. Some psychologists say this is normal and, in some way, they see it as a beneficial instrument. As humans we use blame as an excuse to cover our disappointment, when the outcome is too much to carry or endure. That way we try to get the heavy load of failure off our backs to survive emotionally and press on.

Writer's block and the use of such excuses does not ever happen to me thankfully, because I take full responsibility for achieving the outcome set. One of my strongest preparation rituals includes creating a detailed plan exhibiting my framework of what I'm writing about in each chapter, together with all of the associated key points and examples I will use to convey my messages. Think a MindMap-like document which I've created first, and is sitting right next to my keyboard hence writer's block, passing blame and making excuses is not coming anywhere near my suburb anytime soon.

In fact, I'll know the end result of my planning and preparation will be that I will have a great day writing, truly rewarding. My words will be clearer, my stories more engaging and my use of examples to demonstrate my point will have a far deeper connection to me. What a great feeling it is when I'm truly making inroads with my goals, because I have prepared and planned well in advance, which lies beautifully in line with my WHY and my PURPOSE.

Everything is in sync.

When you least expect it, lurking behind a tree to completely bump you off your plan is the very unwelcoming sight that drags at your heels, trying to break your focus from being in the zone. We talked about it earlier; do not be drawn to shiny objects glistening in the sun which catch the corner of your eye to distract you. If you let 'shiny object syndrome' take over as it tries to force itself onto your list of priorities, it will destroy your best laid plans if you are not strong enough to resist. That is why we need to prioritise all the things we wish to do. When I don't, and if I get stuck inside my own head dealing with overwhelm and anxiety, this builds inside our minds and procrastination sets in and you find it hard to make decisions on what needs to be achieved today. In doing this, because of your underlying sense of overwhelm and the growing anxiety, you begin questioning whether you are making the right choices in your life or not. That's why I know that setting your priorities is so darn important, and why I'm sharing with you the negative aspects of what can occur if you do not focus like a laser on your priorities and goals. The result will be to lose the power to achieve them, just like the power and energy that is created when we placed a magnifying glass in the sun over dry grass in the school ground, just as we remembered at the start of this book.

It is your priorities that will help to:

☑ remove any doubt about where to spend your time

☑ structure days and weeks in a meaningful way, which is always connected with your purpose and your why

☑ say YES or NO when you get requests from others, which take you away from *your* focus and *your* plan.

Ultimately, setting my priorities helps me to set and stick to boundaries, working within the parameters just as I've set in writing this book.

As you've no doubt felt, trying to do *everything* on your to-do list can spread you thin and lead to burnout. So many clients present themselves to me as having a hard time saying NO to others, to projects, tasks and goals which are not directly related to achieving the desired outcomes from hitting your goals.

> '**Responsibility equals accountability equals ownership. And a sense of ownership is the most powerful weapon a team or organisation can have.**'
> *Pat Summitt*

How to set your priorities

Setting your priorities entails identifying what should be done first out of a plethora of priorities all vying for your attention. When everything seems like it should be a top priority and you are constantly pushed for time, panicking to finish to meet the impending deadline. Right now, you feel like you are being stretched too thin; it's difficult to make those key choices in deciding what to do next and what can wait until later.

Planning and effort are required in deciding what should be handled first, and identifying those tasks in a sequential order is the easiest. The MOST urgent should be at the top, the LEAST urgent at the bottom. Prioritisation helps when faced with an overflowing to-do list and constantly moving targets. Time management is critical when setting your priorities, although this can be improved through trial and error, settling down into a comfortable rhythm where you can manage your workflow efficiently and complete more work is the goal.

When you are accomplishing your tasks and you tick those boxes on your to-do list, it gives you peace of mind, personal satisfaction and improves both your reliability and credibility in the workplace.

Create your own to-do list

The first logical step before setting your priorities is to list down all the specific tasks and goals that you want and need to complete. It's great to get a big picture view of your workload from day to day.

It's OK to mix your short-term and long-term activities that you need to complete, but you should separate those onto two separate to-do lists. Remember the differences between the two that were outlined in chapter 1.

Why due dates are a must

On your to-do list, it's important to identify the 'due dates' for the tasks on your list. As we know, a missing due date only ensures that this task is not a priority, so it will never get done.

Did you know the term 'due date' actually relates to pregnancies and the arrival date of your new baby? Interestingly, I find that my clients prefer the term 'due date' much better than the well-used term 'deadline'. I think, for most of us, babies bring happiness – it's a positive word. On the other hand, 'dead' is a sad term which has far more negative connotations. Due Dates it is ...

As an entrepreneur, due dates (yes, deadlines too) are massively critical for assisting you to achieve both short- and long-term goals. However, you won't instantly find success in business by just putting random due dates for all of your tasks, goals and projects. Your due dates are far more important, as they need to set you up for success – they must be strategic.

Due dates linked to strategy, as demonstrated with my book writing goals earlier, are designed to help me move closer to my goals each and every day, each week and each month. Thinking this way, it will keep you clocking up those small but all-important WINS along the way. Even small WINS provide you momentum, and as you build speed you build in stature and along comes a pile of self-belief. Your processes and systems have just been road tested and it gives you proof that it all works. This proof puts a smile of your face, and a spring in your step, racking up a few victories along the way.

It is really imperative to build this momentum along the way. Rather than simply having the image of your big hairy audacious goal, which may be years away, hanging over your head that only adds to your stress levels because you are constantly chasing it. Even still, for most of us, we still worry about due dates – we panic as the date gets closer, only to remind us of our school days cramming for an exam the night before. Remember the sleepless weekend you did in school just to hand in the essay on Monday morning to meet the teacher's due date? What about that crazy few days at work when you and the team needed to put in lots of overtime to finish off that big proposal to win a new client?

As human beings, when we are placed in these prickly situations when the clock is ticking, people get stressed out. When this occurs, we exhibit signs of mood swings, our tempers are shortened and our anxieties are raised, which only adds to the complexity of completing the task before the due date, and working well with the team becomes difficult.

Yet, on the other side of the coin, some people – and I'll raise my hand – just get a singular focus, tunnel vision if you will, and do nothing but work towards achieving that goal with a vigour, contagious enthusiasm and renewed energy, while neglecting other priorities. Such is the engrossing consequences that a due date can have on our working lives.

I get why due dates are really loathed, but there are really good reasons why you should LOVE them. A due date means you're still playing the game and are relevant to the outcome. Got to love that.

Besides, smart organisations use due dates as a source of motivation, inspiration, enthusiasm, and purpose, as opposed to fear. I love the positivity that comes as a result of setting due dates. Set them always, and measure your progress towards achieving them. Make them known and share them with others.

What works for me

Since my time at Apple, planning and prioritisation processes have changed dramatically. We've now got calendar appointments (Google, Outlook), Trello, Monday.com, and Kajabi to add to our go-to favourite: to-do lists.

What I have learned is the best way to take control of your time is to manage your priorities. Here are a few of my go-to personal steps to assist with my priority management. I personally implement these each day as part of my rituals:

☑ **Identify**
Create your weekly to-do list, then I identify which tasks are to be added to your schedule by separating into my 5D's.

✓ **Do**

✓ **Delay**

- ✓ **Delegate**
- ✓ **Delete**
- ✓ **Or contact Darren** (if I'm overwhelmed or don't know where to start)

☑ **Clarify**

I then decide on which day of the week I am going to commence and/or complete each task.

☑ **Organise**

I like to rank my tasks into 1, 2, 3 priorities to determine which tasks are most important and require the most time. My Super To-Do List (see below) works really well, ranking in order of priority.

Remember: 'The best way to manage your time is to take control of your priorities'.

Free download

I've created a **Super To-Do List and my Classic To-Do List** which are popular with my clients.

Please feel free to download from my website.

I've designed these paper-based lists on what works for my clients and have made some simple changes and have created an easy process which they wanted printed as a note pad. Download my FREE Super To-Do and Classic To-Do from: www.tickthoseboxes.com.au/free-stuff/

Create and manage your to-do list

Some of the best to-do lists are not pen-and-paper based, but are online, with some great apps or even better cloud-based software such as: Microsoft Planner, Monday.com, Asana and Trello, and a load more. If you're old-fashioned like me, you could use a simple pen and paper to complete your to-do list, which is truly effective, and I'm happy to debate that with you.

I get asked the question a lot as to what to-do list or project management system should someone use to: manage their time, build the list, track activity and work in progress, and how to maintain to-do tasks. My answer is simple, as I don't really care what application you decide to use, how it's stored, whether cloud based or on your desktop; you must implement whatever works BEST for *you* so you can execute what's required to achieve the task you set out to achieve.

Remember, this is your list, you need to keep it accurately maintained, so you may as well find a system to suit the way you like to work. You are responsible for the way you operate; for me it's a simple pen and paper and my Super To-Do List, in all its simplicity, is the one for me. In all of my private client programs, we offer free access to our group cloud-based Trello Board, so you and my team can keep an eye on your progress to ensure you are comfortably working your way through our sessions together. You have access 24/7, to cater for my clients from around the world operating on different time zones, or if you're local and you get a brain wave in the middle of the night you can work away.

Remember to implement whatever works best for you.

Sort your list

Now that you have written down your to-do list, you need to start analysing it and place things in order.

You can use an app – but again, a traditional pen-and-paper approach using my Super To-Do List works as well as any app. But you may want to consider using apps such as Trello, Asana, Microsoft Planner, Google Sheets, etc. to plot your quadrants.

When you have doubt about correctly setting your priorities, and you are not sure when or how you should attack a task or goal, it's usually time to roll out my trusty and proven 5D process first. You can also revisit the Eisenhower Matrix. This first cut takes away those items which are NOT important really quickly, so you can avoid overwhelm and doubt.

Then, you can place the remaining tasks in a sequential order to work on the most important first.

5D's to Get Sh!t Done – it's GSD time

Apply my 5D's – five actions you can revert to immediately upon struggling to reach a clear decision.

Do

'Just Do It'... love this, but that belongs to Nike.

You've reached the decision to do it, you're all in – excellent. So, you'll put your maximum effort into getting it done before the deadline if you are like me, otherwise completely on the deadline works too. So long as you make a commitment and you honour it.

'The difference between "engagement" and "commitment" is like an egg and bacon breakfast: the chicken was "involved" but the pig was "committed".'

You must first truly invest yourself in a goal, task or project for it to be successful. There's no halfway. Why, you ask?

Because you can't afford to be there not present and not fully engaged. Merely *participating,* strolling through the motions, means you're not committed enough, and if you're not committed enough, what you've been working on won't come to light ...

By the way, you can't work on multiple tasks at once and expect excellent results. Do one task and do it well. Invest everything you have in getting it accurate, then you can move on to the next task armed with that renewed success and spring in your step that you get from achieving your goal, ticking that box and putting a big smile on your face.

Multitasking, which was the buzzword for many employees and business owners during the early 2000s and I must divulge, has been my arch nemesis for many years. Suzi, my wife, often reminds me that 'I cannot multitask successfully', and she's absolutely right. I must positively focus on doing ONE thing at a time. Getting that precise and producing my best work means I play my best game, then moving onto the next project or task, and she is unquestionably correct.

Doing too many things at once has never worked for me. It's pleasing to know that it's not just me fumbling my way through. The successful author and educational consultant Kendra Cherry is focused on helping students learn about psychology and she has written an awesome blog to answer the question 'Does Multitasking Make You More Productive'?

Kendra writes, 'Take a moment and think about all the things you are doing right now. Obviously, you are reading this blog (or chapter 3 of my book), but chances are pretty darn high that you are also doing several things at once. Perhaps you're also listening to music, texting a friend, checking your email in another browser tab, or playing a computer game.'

According to Kendra, 'If you are doing several things at once, then you may be what researchers refer to as a 'heavy multitasker.' And you probably think you are fairly proficient at this balancing act. According to numerous studies, you are probably 'not as effective as you think you are'.

'Research has demonstrated that switching from one task to the next takes a serious toll on productivity. Multitaskers have more trouble tuning out distractions than people who focus on one task at a time. Also, doing so many things at once can actually impair cognitive ability.'

'To determine the impact of multitasking, psychologists asked study participants to switch tasks and then measured how much time was lost by switching. In one study conducted by Robert Rogers and Stephen Monsell, participants were slower when they had to switch tasks than when they repeated the same task.'

Another study, by Joshua Rubinstein, Jeffrey Evans, and David Meyer, found that 'participants lost significant amounts of time as they switched between multiple tasks and lost even more time as the tasks became increasingly complex'.

For me, I'm an all-in guy who has learnt from my past activities, those which haven't always worked out the way I'd like, and others, completed to my absolute satisfaction and ticked those boxes. Knowing what works best for me means I set my target and off I go ... embracing the essence of Nike's iconic 'Just Do It' slogan.

Personally, I feel there are no three better placed words used to describe; if you have something you desire to do, and you have evaluated it as something that will benefit you, then stop wasting valuable time and energy: JUST DO IT.

Delay

Delay is something you can't do until you learn how to do it, then it's a good idea. My gut tells me it's also the right thing to do as there's nothing worse than allocating the time needed to complete a task or goal but you struggle to do because you don't know how to complete it correctly. No, it's not a procrastination element, for me it's the opposite.

It's tolerable to delay a task or goal because we don't consider we have the competence to do a task correctly or make a decision which impacts others until all the data is in hand.

Procrastination or 'intentional delay'? Procrastination hinders many business owners, their execs and teams, but sometimes delaying work to plan ahead or gather more data can be beneficial.

Delegate

Have someone else do something you can't do. Delegation helps not only the manager or owner of the company keep good business order but also helps employees to feel important and responsible for their own actions and responsibilities ... Delegating tasks to employees is a fine way to motivate the team and keep them moving up in your business.

It's healthy for you and the entire organisation to delegate a task or goal to another person who is better placed to complete it.

Perhaps it's to a subject matter expert or a thought leader in the particular topic, so it's beneficial as it delegates a task to another person who has a particular interest in the area who you are sure will do a better job at completing the task that you will do. After all, the achievement of the desired outcome is what's important. Remember, if there are tasks that could be taken charge of by someone else, then delegate.

Don't mistake delegation for running away from your responsibilities. Delegation is an important function of management.

Make sure whomever you delegate the task to has the skill, capacity, ability and time to get it done by the deadline.

As a business owner, you will need to learn the art of delegating work to specific team members based on their efficiency level. Just a tip based on my past mistakes, so lucky I'm a good learner. Make sure you do not to turn something you delegate into a boomerang that's going to hit when you least expect it on its way back. The worst pitfall of delegating is having to do double the work when you discover that several tasks have not been done well, so setting expectations is critical and will save you time later. It's easier to make sure your brief is concise and your expectations are clearly known and understood by the person you are delegating to. If not, be assured it will come back to bite you – it always does.

Delete

There is immense pleasure to be had by deleting a task or goal that has been set by another person which is not aligned to your purpose, your why, and it's not within your own key performance indicators. Now let's be practical here, we should be helping others out; it's good karma and good business, and I'm always the first to put up my hand to offer assistance and support, so mastering the ability to selectively delete will require some learning of how to filter through your task list and not piss off others. Remember that what's a priority for others is not necessarily a priority for you. Learning how to professionally deal with this is important when you are focusing on your goals and your tasks and being held to account for them.

Deleting irrelevant emails on your inbox is an example of what I'm talking about. Junk or spam mail deserves to be sent straight to the recycling bin if they're cluttering up your inbox. For tasks that you still need to accomplish, double check if you still need to complete them. Take them off your to-do list if you don't.

You should also learn how to say NO to certain tasks. Review your existing list before agreeing to take on extra work. Refuse politely in case you aren't equipped to add more tasks to your current workflow.

Call – your Accountability Partner or Buddy

Okay, so this is a 'D' because when I work with my clients it's 'contact Darren'.

Having a person to reach out to for a priority check, perhaps a priority realignment, is often needed.

Review your workload and to-do list regularly and pick any item, then get stuck into it. If you're feeling positive and in a good headspace, then grab the hardest task on your to-do list and get it done. Strangle that sucker, and tick it off your list... Good on you for picking the hardest task as you know it gets easier from here on, with the hardest now being done and dusted. How good does that feel!

If you're feeling sluggish and not ready to fight with Rocky for another few rounds, then pick the easier task on your to-do list and get it done. Nothing wrong with getting into a routine of picking a task and smashing it. Just getting into a rhythm of completing tasks puts you in a better headspace and frame of mind to take on the harder tasks and get through your to-do's.

Is there one task that always ends up at the bottom of the pile? If you find you're avoiding it, ask yourself and those in your team if there's somebody else to do it, or can you delay it until you have time? Perhaps you can delegate it to someone who has the time to do it now, maybe they have a special interest or subject-matter expertise in this field, maybe their time is better used by attending to this task and your time is better spent doing other things? Could it be their job to do it, or can you give an eager team member an opportunity to step up and take this task off your hands? We all know a good stretch of capability is a great opportunity to learn, grow, make mistakes and get out of a comfort zone.

'Accountability' is a powerful word, yet most don't know what it means. For most of us, that 'A' word sends a shiver up our spines, yet most don't know what it really means, and nor can they spell it correctly.

What we do know is that we must 'step up' and be responsible for something. Accountability means delivering on a promise or honouring a commitment made to others and to ourselves. You see, there is a difference between Accountability and Responsibility, they are cousins, but not the same.

Let me explain. **We are responsible for things and accountable to people.** Accountability entails keeping promises or honouring commitments made to ourselves or others.

There is a distinction to be made between accountability and responsibility; they are cousins rather than siblings.

Responsibility refers to the duties and obligations we have to complete tasks or achieve goals. It is the state of being in charge of something and is often linked to a specific role or position.

For example, a project manager is responsible for ensuring that a project is completed on time and within budget.

Accountability, on the other hand, refers to the willingness to take responsibility for our actions and decisions. It is the act of answering for our actions, both to ourselves and to others.

Accountability involves being answerable for the outcomes of our choices and decisions. For example, a project manager may be held accountable for the success or failure of a project.

In summary, responsibility refers to the tasks or goals we are responsible for, while accountability refers to the consequences of our actions and decisions.

Responsibility – *is about what we are tasked to do.*

Accountability – *is about taking ownership of the results.*

So it is essential that if we want to get stuff done we will need a person with whom we can work, someone in a central role to hold you to account.

Accountability increases Activity + Activity increases Opportunity.

Let me to introduce you to Tracy Angwin

I have recorded a Zoom session with Tracy, who is a solutions expert, media commentator and popular keynote speaker and the driving force behind the Australian Payroll Association.

Tracy is also the bestselling author of *The Payroll Revolution* (2013), *Profit from Payroll* (2015) and *In Safe Hands: How to Make Payroll Outsourcing Work for You* (2017). She is often asked by media to give commentary and guidance on all aspects of payroll, including why employers get payroll wrong, how to optimise the payroll function, and what is the future of payroll.

Tracy's full bio appears below.

Bonus video

Watch the video recording of my full interview with Tracy conducted over Zoom, due to COVID restrictions and stage-4 isolation at the time of recording, on my website. Please visit: www.tickthoseboxes.com.au/TheAccountabilityAdvantage

Here's my discussion with Tracy.

DARREN: Tell me about what happened to a group of restaurants that was created by George Calombaris, the celebrity TV chef and judge on *Masterchef*? Was his demise due to a lack of accountability?

TRACY ANGWIN: I think certainly a lack of oversight. What we find happens in not just that situation but all the underpayment issues that we've been involved with (we weren't involved with the Calombaris team, but a lot of them that you see in the paper we are), the problem is this whole set-and-forget mentality, or set-and-neglect as we call it in the office. You set up payroll technology just once and assume that it continues to work. Which is fine if things never change, and if it was set up correctly in the first place.

DARREN: You read the newspapers, you've seen the headlines. You know the truth behind some of the claims of underpayments to staff by some companies, so what do you understand the term 'accountability' to mean?

TRACY ANGWIN: It's probably more so in my team and my clients that I think about accountability. Certainly, from a client point of view, I believe there's got to be more accountability. But I think very well you can sort of throw the accountability term around. You've got to have some sort of infrastructural planning or system to hold people accountable, because it shouldn't be a negative thing.

DARREN: It's interesting you raise that, because as an Accountability Coach I find that some people's first impression is accountability leads to punishment, like that you made a promise to your team members and didn't deliver on it. Many people see it as a negative. They don't see that accountability is a positive superpower, all-encompassing event that if you do it right, you bring a whole lot of people along for a ride. It's not just on one person.

TRACY ANGWIN: I was going to wear your T-shirt ... it is that, *Getting Stuff Done (GSD or Die).*

DARREN: It is, and we all need more of that in our lives and our businesses. As a leader of your very entrepreneurial business, but also as the CEO of Australian Payroll, you've got many members who see you as their leader; how do you hold yourself to account?

TRACY ANGWIN: For me, everything I do needs to be defendable. I think about it quite a lot because I'm not averse to being controversial, I'm quite happy to call out things publicly. But I always need to make sure – my worst fear is to call something out and be wrong. So, I just make sure that when I do something, particularly if I do it publicly, it's completely defendable and I've got the evidence to back it up.

The Tracy Angwin story

A self-described 'corporate escapee with an obsession for improving payroll compliance and efficiency', Tracy is a big-picture industry innovator on multiple fronts.

As founder and CEO of the Australian Payroll Association, which provides payroll advisory services as well as payroll training and qualifications, she delivers thought leadership to the industry, employers and partners.

She is the host of the 'Talking Payroll' podcast, available on iTunes, Soundcloud and at www.austpayroll.com.au.

Tracy is driven by a belief that payroll is a business-critical function that can have devastating financial and emotional consequences if botched. It is impossible to have a high-performing, motivated and engaged workforce if payroll isn't correct and delivered on time.

Tracy is on a mission to help employers get payroll right.

As a thought leader in the field, Tracy's efforts have led to Australia's first nationally accredited payroll qualifications, the Certificate IV in Payroll Administration and Diploma of Payroll

Management. These qualifications are part of the Australian Qualifications Framework, and pave the way for the payroll industry to finally lift its professional standards and attract new talent.

> **'Ninety-nine percent of all failures come from people who have a habit of making excuses.'**
> *George Washington Carver*

Chapter 4

Plan what needs to be done and how you will do it

Moves you to 50% – if you plan how you will do it.

50%

The Road to Accountability

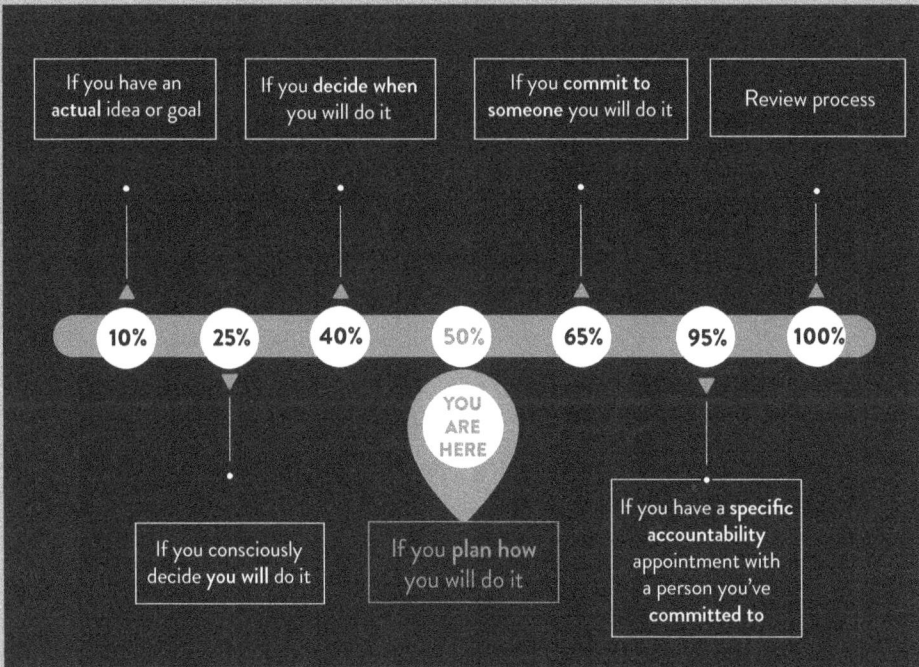

If you have an **actual** idea or goal — 10%

If you **decide when** you will do it — 25%

If you consciously decide **you will** do it — 40%

If you **plan how** you will do it — 50% (YOU ARE HERE)

If you **commit to someone** you will do it — 65%

If you have a **specific accountability** appointment with a person you've **committed to** — 95%

Review process — 100%

Based on the 2010 study conducted by the American Society of Training and Development (ASTD).

To achieve your **goals**, you need to truly commit yourself. That is, never lose sight of what you want to achieve. You think about it when you wake up and think about it before you fall asleep. This chapter *moves you to 50% – if you plan how you will do it.*

> ### 'A goal without a plan is just a wish.'
> *Antoine de Saint-Exupéry*

Understand the importance of planning, put a thought process down before you start anything, and use your time to your advantage. Remember, the idea is always to reduce the total amount of time that you are working in half, or even more.

In this chapter, we'll cover:

☑ Scheduling your tasks.

☑ Evaluating your progress.

☑ Common pitfalls and why you may fail.

Planning is indispensable for business success. You simply cannot reach a goal without implementing and executing on a plan – winging it does not work. It may work in the short term for a specific task, but not when you are trying to achieve big goals in the longer term.

Of course, planning alone will not yield a result; you then need to work diligently to be successful.

> ### 'Accountability separates the wishers in life from the action-takers that care enough about their future to account for their daily actions.'
> *John Di Lemme*

Planning is essential because it provides clarity. It also reduces the overall vision into what needs to be done, which is an essential step for turning the plan into execution. It also helps find out key issues in the business early on, including obstacles, possible pitfalls and areas which haven't been looked into. Business planning helps you improve your work productivity by ensuring that you are on the right track to achieve your goals. It also helps you predict the blockage that you may get in your business success, which helps to provide the solution to the problem you will face in the future.

Organisation planning

Planning helps an organisation design a course to achieve its goals. Like any formal organisation process, it should start with a review of the organisation's ongoing activities to define:

- ☑ Exactly where is the organisation right now?

- ☑ Where does the organisation need to be at a specific time; say 30 days, maybe it's end of the quarter, half year or on an annual basis.

- ☑ What's stopping the organisation from getting there?

- ☑ What's the plan for how the organisation will get there?

- ☑ Why is it so important for the organisation to get there in the first place?

- ☑ What's the motivating factor? This is the organisation's WHY and purpose.

Ideally, this will be where you rally your team to share the same goal, and where you work together with laser focus to implement and execute to achieve the goals that you have set. And you will define the small steps required to achieve BIG.

Let's consider some of the key issues you will need to understand when you are planning.

Efficient use of resources

All organisations, big and small, have limited resources. The planning process provides the information that top management needs to make effective decisions about how your assets – people, intellectual property, financial resources – are distributed to enable the organisation to achieve its goals. With good planning, productivity is maximised, and resources are not wasted on projects with a low probability of success or low return on investment.

Establishing organisational goals

The aim is to set goals that challenge everyone in the organisation. This is key to getting buy in and support from everyone. Individuals striving for better performance are one of the key facets of any planning process.

Goals must be aggressive, but realistic and a stretch. Businesses must not be content with how they are doing at the moment, or they are likely to lose ground to their competitors. I remember my late father-in-law, the entrepreneurial Hal Levy, telling me 'my competition is good, you have to be better'. So, now it's time to lift your game and up the ante, taking it to yet another level. Wonderful advice ... thanks Hal.

Another advantage of creating a goal is that the forecast results are compared with the actual results to hold whomever is responsible to account, thus creating full accountability. Organisations analyse significant deviations from projections and take action to address situations where revenues are lower than planned or spending is higher. The process of setting goals and targets can be a wake-up call for complacent managers.

Managing risk and uncertainty

Risk management is crucial for the success of an organisation. Even the biggest companies cannot control the economic and competitive environment around them. A notable example is the mobile phone market. Did Motorola predict the rise of Nokia? Did Nokia see the emergence of Blackberry? Did Apple have any idea of the rise of Samsung? And so, it goes on. As I write this book, another organisation is planning its leapfrog over Apple to get to the top. Who will emerge? What's going to be their point of difference? I wonder what their unique selling proposition will look like? Unforeseen events that occur must be dealt with quickly, before negative financial consequences of these events become severe.

Think about where we are today. Why did governments and health organisations not prepare properly for this pandemic? Why were they NOT ready for COVID-19? Just take look at the death toll and financial ruin it has caused across the world.

Planning encourages the development of 'what-if' scenarios, in which managers identify potential risk factors and progress emergency plans to deal with them.

The pace of change in business is rapid, and organisations must be in a position to quickly modify their strategies to suit the changing conditions of the time.

Consider the COVID business pivot to reinvent and reset. The pivot has become necessary as 'a do or die' choice for the survival of some organisations during this time of high uncertainty. For those doing exactly this, I take my hat off to your courage and survival.

Team building and cooperation

Planning encourages team building and the spirit of cooperation. When the plan is finalised and communicated to the members of the organisation, everyone knows their designated responsibilities, are clear on how other areas of the organisation need their support and expertise to accomplish the assigned tasks. It's important that individual team members can see how their specific contributions all add up to collectively make a difference to the overall success of the organisation.

Consider having your team build the strategy and plan to achieve the specific goal. That way, your team members will take ownership for the results and push for success.

Potential conflicts can be reduced if the top management asks for the input of department or divisional heads during the goal-setting process. Individuals are less resentful of fiscal targets if they have had a say in their creation.

Creating competitive advantages

Planning helps organisations to have a realistic view of their current strengths and weaknesses compared to major competitors. The management team identifies areas where clients can be better served, by truly understanding the client's needs, identifying and solving the client's problems. Then sharp businesses build strategies to develop products, offerings and solutions which offer meaningful and well-considered solutions to problems.

Measuring your progress

There are several methods to measure progress, and here are four ways you can approach it:

1 **Process objectives.** To give an example, if you want to generate more revenue, the critical processes you choose may include pitches or suggestions, customer conversations, or telephone calls with interested parties.

   It's critical that you specifically measure the appropriate processes, whether they be based on time, quality, cost, or outcomes.

2 **Reflect on how far you have travelled.** It can be very motivating to look back to where you started and acknowledge how far you have come, especially when your results are starting to flourish.

3 **Estimate the remaining distance to reach the goals.** This is an alternative way to establish progress by estimating how far you still need to travel to reach your goals. It's likely to be helpful not to do this when the goals are too distant, as this might prove to be demoralising.

4 **Regular follow-up.** Define measurements of progress. It can be an effective means of holding yourself accountable while ensuring transparency as you approach your objectives.

Setting goals and measuring progress is a tremendous instrument to keep the journey on track, and in my experience, it is so much more difficult and virtually impossible to accurately improve what you cannot measure in the first place. Taking a guess is not sufficient.

Common pitfalls and why you may fail

I've been engaged as an Accountability Coach for business owners, executives and their teams to work on a broad selection of topics and different industries and sectors from all parts of the globe. All have similar requirements, and the common objectives from our meetings are to work together to improve skills, solve problems and to take advantage of and create opportunities.

In coaching that many people from so many different backgrounds representing a diversified array of sectors, industries and groups, I've realised there are seven genuine and legitimate reasons why people *don't* **G**et **S**tuff **D**one.

Let us not confuse them with the self-important stories often used to justify one's own situation. These are not excuses, nor is it an apportionment of blame, but legitimate and genuine circumstances that truly stop people from moving forward in a positive fashion.

These are real and genuine scenarios from boardrooms and home offices all over the world that impede one's ability to proceed forward, on the road to accountability.

> **'You are the reason of your own good-luck and bad-luck; success and failure; happiness and pain. Your choices are responsible for your present. Don't blame someone else for your sufferings or failures.'**
> *Sanjeev Himachali*

Here's my Top Seven reasons why people don't Get Sh!t Done

How many apply to you?

1. Feeling overwhelmed

You have too much to focus on at once so you give your attention to whatever yells the loudest.

Solutions:

- ☑ Write down everything that is demanding your attention right now – take the 'overwhelm' out of your head and put it on paper, where you can distance yourself from it a bit. Write down every task you can think of that you are worrying about.

- ☑ Create bite-sized chunks – once you've written everything down, group your tasks and to-dos into smaller chunks.

Organising your to-do's into smaller chunks will help you see your world more clearly and lighten the mental load.

☑ Choose carefully – look at your chunks and prioritise your to-do's based on what makes you feel strong. Which ones do you love? Which ones are you actually looking forward to?

☑ Grab those and make a plan to do these first, and to find a small way to celebrate them when you've done them. If possible, delegate to others who have interest or expertise to offer.

☑ Organising and managing these activities will give you strength and resilience to get through everything else.

☑ Take action – action is the best antidote to feeling overwhelmed. Just begin. Very often the simple action of beginning will alleviate the anxiety and stress that has accumulated.

☑ Focus – on the task at hand. Think about what you are doing rather than what you're not getting done. Worry and time have a special relationship. The more you have of one, the less you have of the other. Both are suspended when you simply focus on what is in front of you right now.

2. Being over-ambitious

People try to get too much done in an unrealistic time frame. Often, this is because they cannot say NO to others.

Solutions:

☑ You must review your schedule and your plans to see if you can actually physically accommodate a new deadline. If it places too much of a squeeze on you, say NO and delegate to others, or reset the deadline so you can fit it in when it suits you.

☑ Don't forget to also consider the emotional energy required to complete this task. Ensure you are not left drained after giving your all to complete this task. Running on empty *always* catches up with you.

☑ Remember my 5D's? (Do, Delay, Delegate, Delete, or call Darren.)

☑ Ambition addicts; you have a really hard time relaxing and winding down. Often you feel that unscheduled time fills you with dread. You find it challenging to enjoy simple pleasures such as relaxing in the evening as you only have two speeds; flat out and off. If you must unwind, you prefer to do so through competitive activities or quantifiable hobbies where winning is the goal.

   Ambition addicts – free yourselves from this anxiety and allow for some vulnerability. When life presents you with loose ends, bewilderment, fragilities and failure, you ambition addicts can become irrational and flustered. Learn to relax. Not everything is a competition, and you don't have to be operating at 200% every minute of every day.

3. Having NO plan

You want to do a certain task or project, but you are not in the suitable mindset to create a plan that works. Some folks never create plans for anything, they merely piece together many band-aid solutions on the fly – which is not sustainable or effective in the long term – and hope like crazy that it works.

> **'If you fail to plan; you are planning to fail.'**
> *Benjamin Franklin*

Love that quote. There's never a been truer statement, particularly on your road to accountability. Sage advice indeed.

Solutions:

☑ Whenever you plan, you plan to succeed. So, it is not a surprise that planning will eventually lead you to have more success and achieve a better position in the market, be it a brand or a product.

☑ If you are planning to succeed, the plan will include tracking your progress as well as the best pathway to achieve the goal.

☑ Planning is important, because through tracking progress, an integrated approach, flexibility, and all of the other points mentioned above, planning ultimately helps the individual reach a desired point in a timely fashion.

4. The weight of past problems

Whatever has stopped you from achieving things in the past is still present. Your monkey is still on your back, and you don't have a plan to deal with it – hoping it will go away, but you know it won't. You may not be able to move on from a past failure or criticism, or you may be weighed down by fear and anxiety that stop you moving forward.

Solutions:

☑ Things don't disappear on their own. You need to make the commitment to 'let it go'. If you don't make this conscious choice up front, you could end up self-sabotaging any effort to move on from this past hurt.

☑ In every moment, you have that choice – to continue to feel bad about the past, or to start feeling good. You need to take responsibility for your own happiness, and not put such power into the hands of a past event.

☑ Now it's time to let go. Let go of the past, and stop reliving it. Stop telling yourself you can't do this. You can't undo the past; all you can do is make today the best day of your life.

5. You don't know where to start

You don't know where to start the exercise, so you procrastinate and never actually begin.

Solutions:

☑ Procrastination is the greatest robber of self-confidence. It eats away at you and makes you feel bad about yourself.

☑ Focus is the greatest enhancer of self-confidence, so if you're stuck, forget about the big picture – just focus on taking the first step.

☑ Remember this gold from Keith Abraham CSP: 'the day you take the first step of the task you have been procrastinating about – the task that may be holding you back – is the day you beat procrastination.'

☑ Idea gremlins show up and disrupt the soul without explanation. If you try to figure them out before it's time, it will only end in frustration. Instead, let them come. Let them dance. Let them turn over some tables and make a mess. See what they have to say without demanding they have a reason. But don't let them take over.

☑ If you want to start or finish a project which has no name and no structure as yet, so it's basically invisible except inside your head, it's imperative to get it down on paper and listen to feedback from others. Formulate that into a living, breathing object which is no longer just floating as an idea but rather it's now on paper and it exists. It's real in every sense of the word; now it's your intellectual property, which even has laws to protect it as your creation.

6. You don't have a big enough reason

You don't have a big enough reason to get the task or project done, so there's NO true motivation to get it completed. Usually you move on to the next project while leaving the current one unfinished, because this project has no real reason why you should focus on completing it and finishing it. It's not aligned with your WHY or your purpose, so there is no genuine and authentic connection.

Solutions:

☑ Share the project or task with someone and ask them to keep you accountable. That way, there's a lot more at stake if you don't get it done. You won't want to let them down too, will you?

☑ Better understand WHY you need to complete this project or task, so you will understand the importance of the role you play and how your completion (or not) impacts others. Understand the BIG picture.

☑ I can find lots of procrastination techniques to keep me from reaching the finish line. That's when I take a few minutes to visualise what it means to be finished with the project. Then I push hard to power through and get it done.

7. No one cares

You have no one to hold YOU accountable, so the deadline passes without fuss ... it's as if no one cares. However, if you agreed on a completion date with someone else, that person would check your progress and help you get through the challenging moments and help you get over that finish line to meet your deadline and commitment.

Solutions:

☑ Sometimes you just can't do it alone, so swallow that pride and ask for some help – suck it up. Others will have different ideas on how to complete the project better and more quickly. It also brings in a fresh set of eyes and experiences to the task or project, which can only provide positive benefits for all, with healthier outcomes. So much to gain from sharing with others.

☑ Ask someone you trust to check in with you on your progress, and create a timeline to ensure you are on track.

☑ Engage an Accountability Partner, Coach or Buddy who will keep you on track so you keep those promises and commitments made to others and to yourself. Choosing the right person is key and they will get you to 95% probability on our road to accountability.

Let me introduce you to Rob Nankervis

I have recorded a Zoom session with Rob, who shares with us his experiences in working with the senior leaders of some of the largest organisations in Australia. Rob works with the big end of town, working with organisations with annual turnovers of between $2m and $500m, as their Business Coach focusing on scalability. Rob is also an acknowledged entrepreneur and author in his own right. I hope you enjoy our chat.

Rob's full bio appears below.

Bonus video

Watch the video recording of my full interview with Rob conducted over Zoom, due to COVID restrictions and stage-4 isolation at the time of recording, on my website. Please visit: www.tickthoseboxes.com.au/TheAccountabilityAdvantage

Here's my discussion with Rob.

DARREN: When you go to an organisation, how do you start the process?

ROB NANKERVIS: The first thing is really trying to find out what the owner, founder and leaders are trying to achieve. What would good look like to them in say three to five years? What would good look like in 10 or 15 years? And then, where are they now against that desire? Then what we try to do is say: well, we're really about addressing the gap between where you are now and where you'd like this to be, particularly in the medium term (three- to five-year period).

DARREN: How much of that direction do those clients give you, and is that often related to a financial achievement or are there other components that are non-monetary?

ROB NANKERVIS: It's a number of things. I've had a number of people in the last three or four months that are say $20–$25 million businesses who say they want to be $50–$75 million. $50 million businesses want to be 100. I've been helping a couple of $200 million businesses that want to be in the $400–$500 million range. So, for those sorts of businesses there is a metric they are holding up to say: this is what would represent success. Then you can ask questions like: if you are $25 million now and you want to get to 50, where is the other 25 coming from? And that becomes the strategy, because effectively doubling in three years means 25% growth year-on-year. So, what strategies do you need to put in place, what execution disciplines and so on to deliver on that kind of growth trajectory? So that fosters that sort of discussion.

The other part might be: look, we'd like to exit or we'd like to list the company, or we'd like to have a multistate operation. There are many of these that the ambitions get realised.

DARREN: Do they often come with multiple ambitions?

ROB NANKERVIS: Yeah. They obviously don't want it to look like a small business; they'd like it to be bigger and more profitable and more valuable. And sometimes to be more profitable you've got to reinvest. There potentially will be a soft patch where you can invest in to make it more profitable in a couple of years' time, but you've got to wear some of it now.

DARREN: What's the process you go through to prioritise? You do want to get these ambitions into some level of what to do first and second ... how do you do that exercise?

ROB NANKERVIS: I'll tend to talk to people about the front domino. You know, in a game of dominoes you can tap all sorts of dominoes, but which is the domino that if you tap will tap most other dominoes? And sometimes it's been about wall charting. You know, getting sticky notes and saying: well, we are on the left-hand side of the chart today; out on the right-hand side of the chart would be this many people, this much revenue, this kind of market coverage – the sandbox we'll be applying will look like this. How does that plan map out on a three-year butcher's paper across the wall and where do all those pieces need to go? And that's been a very visual way for some teams to actually realise firstly how frontloaded their thinking is in terms of: we've got a pretty good view of the next six months or maybe a year; but really there is a lot of vacant space in years 2 and 3. It also speaks to how well they understand the interrelationship between the goals they've got. You know, if we are going to be expanding the business can we really expand into America and into Asia at the same time? Have we got the money, the time and resources and so on to tackle those multiple goals? Does that make sense? Does it make sense in a risk perspective, for example, as well?

So, these are the sorts of things that they map out. And usually, we try and get them to corral those into about five strategic things, you know, a handful of things that are going to make the most difference.

DARREN: Rob, this is absolute gold. I appreciate the time that you've given me today and to share this with all of our viewers. I wonder if you remember that wonderful email you sent me about the six C's. Do you want to just share those with us and explain those six C's? I think it's a wonderful way to round up our whole conversation we've had this morning.

ROB NANKERVIS: Sure. In terms of some tips for helping drive accountability throughout the business, the first thing is **clarity**. Get really clear about the direction of the business. It's effectively the strategic point – what needs to be done? Then against that, the second C about **commitment**. What is the commitment to the priorities that are going to deliver on those strategies? And get that commitment down to an individual. Third one is **colours**. What would green look like on doing this? What's done? And then in terms of checking in on the dones, what's the **cadence** – that regular meeting rhythm that you're going to institute in the business? And we go from kind of annual planning right down to 12-minute daily huddles for everybody in the business. They would know that's the cadence. What about **coaching** then for the individual, as well as that cross commitment? What's the individual coaching follow-up, either peer coaching between individuals in a business, or boss and direct report accountability to help keep them on track with the handful of things they've committed for the month and the quarter? And then, what's the **celebration**? On a couple of levels, how are people measuring things so that they can tell themselves that they've had a good month, week, quarter? And so, is there something bigger for the business or for that division? You know, they've just implemented the new accounting system, they've won four new accounts, they've got all the trees planted for the coming horticultural season – what way are you going to celebrate this before you start that cycle again?

The Rob Nankervis story

Growing up, Rob spent most weekends at the wharf watching his father manage the team at the transport and storage company he worked at, teaching him the foundations of great leadership and the importance of culture.

Passionate about business, Rob decided to pursue a degree in accounting at Victoria University and landed several financial roles across major Australian organisations News Corporation, Peter MacCallum Institute and the Australian Wheat Board.

A few years later, Rob was selected by SMS Management & Technology for a consultancy role, where he led a practice and worked alongside the CEO in the area of relationship management.

During his nine-year stint, he helped the company achieve significant growth, most of which was attributed to the strength of the culture within the organisation. This experience inspired Rob to learn more about leadership and gain a deeper understanding of what it took to build a great company culture.

Not long after, he was head-hunted by Oppeus International for the role of Strategic Leadership Advisor, becoming a client partner and part owner in just a few short years.

He then went on to lead a team of senior managers at Ernst & Young as a Director of Performance Improvement across the health, transport and defence industries.

After serving over 30 years in the corporate world, gaining a lifetime of experience and being passionate about developing the next generation of leaders, Rob felt like it was finally time to venture out on his own.

That's when he founded Propelling Performance, a boutique leadership advisory firm working with mid-tier leaders to increase profitability through strategic action and high-performance teams.

Rob's personalised one-to-one coaching, public workshops and keynote presentations help to solve the common challenges Senior Executives face in driving growth and performance. Rob is currently the Managing Director of Propelling Performance, which was founded in 2013 as a boutique leadership advisory firm, on a mission to help build the next generation of leaders.

Through personalised team-based and one-to-one coaching, public workshops and keynote presentations, Rob helps to solve the common challenges senior executives and organisations face in their day-to-day roles. This includes business growth, team culture, operational performance and cash flow. Rob does this by redefining organisations, strategic direction, values and goals, to pinpoint the priorities the company needs to focus on for effective performance and delivering growth.

Rob is a Certified Coach in the well-known 'Scaling Up' methodology developed by Verne Harnish. He is also credentialled as a Level 2 Organisational Coach through the IECL.

He is committed to working with senior executives who are contemplating driving sustainable growth and increased profitability through strategic action and high-performing teams.

'The price of greatness is responsibility.'
Winston Churchill

Chapter 5

Tell the world

Moves you to 65% – if you commit to someone you will do it.

65%

The Road to Accountability

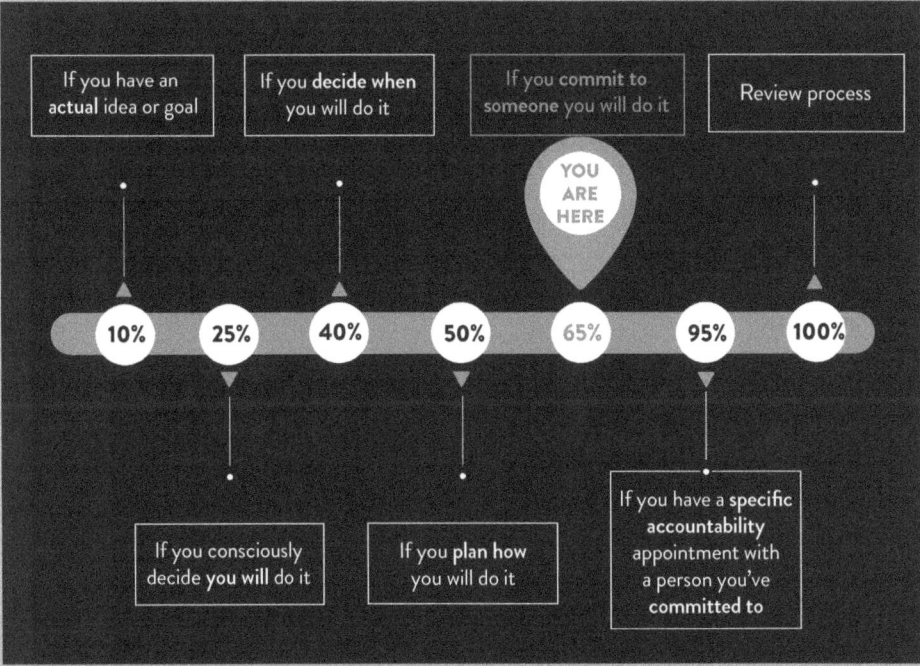

If you have an **actual** idea or goal

If you **decide when** you will do it

If you commit to someone you will do it

Review process

YOU ARE HERE

10% 25% 40% 50% 65% 95% 100%

If you consciously decide **you will** do it

If you **plan how** you will do it

If you have a **specific accountability** appointment with a person you've **committed to**

Based on the 2010 study conducted by the American Society of Training and Development (ASTD).

The Accountability Advantage

Telling the entire world about your goal, your task or project moves you to *65% probability of achieving your goal – if you commit to someone you will do it*. This moves you nicely along our road of accountability.

Naturally it makes sense for you to find the tallest building, and to scream your intentions loudly and clearly from the top. Geez, if I were totally committed to achieving a goal that I'd set, then I would. Hell yeah, I'd climb over walls and break through all the barriers that were stopping me from achieving what I'd planned and prioritised to achieve.

The importance of committing to someone else, other than yourself, to hold you accountable for the goals you set is fundamentally the foundation of being held to account.

In this chapter, we'll cover three key components:

☑   Who should you share your goals with?

☑   The ins and outs of Accountability Partners.

☑   When to share your goals.

You are now in the intermediate phase of the road to accountability, where you feel the environment starting to change; both on emotional and physical levels, you begin to detect that momentum is on moving onto your side.

We love momentum, it pulls you forward and keeps the train rolling in the right direction, and armed with this forward momentum it's not the time to take your foot of the accelerator. In fact, keep it firmly planted as you have still got a way to go on our road to accountability.

To maintain that positive wave of emotion and action, you need to be accountable to yourself. The simplest way to accomplish this and to tick those boxes is to find someone that can hold you accountable. Life is complex, and so is the human mind and emotions. To try to conquer it on your own is a recipe for disaster, a statement we know is backed by the 2010 study on the probability of achieving your goals which found that 95% probability can be achieved – if you have a *specific* accountability appointment with a person you've *committed* to.

Let's explore the importance of committing to someone else, other than yourself, to hold you accountable for the goals you set. Remember, the idea is to achieve all of the goals you set for yourself. Overcoming the anxiety and scattered energy to get there can be aided with the guidance of someone who can hold you accountable.

> **'Understanding the true meaning of accountability makes us strong and enables us to learn.'**
> *Sameh Elsayed*

Who should you share your goals with?

Goal setting, in itself, can be an individual process. It is a reflection of the things you have done, and also a vision of the things you want to do. It is an energetic process that can catapult your life forward.

It thus may seem counter-intuitive to share these goals with someone else, but there is tremendous power in doing so!

Research by Ohio State University backs the argument that sharing your goals with someone else is effective, BUT it has to be with someone 'whose opinion you respect' or who is 'higher in status'. This means careful selection is required.

In this instance, it may mean sharing it with people in the following positions:

☑ an Accountability Partner or Buddy

☑ a mentor or coach

☑ family, friends

☑ manager, colleagues or your cohort

☑ go tell the world; the more people that know, the better.

Accountability Partner, Coach or a Buddy

Accountability, without a doubt, increases your motivation levels and ability to focus. You are starting to hear more about Accountability Partners, also known as an Accountability Buddy, because they really make a difference in how entrepreneurs, executives and the broader business community achieve their goals, while we all strive to achieve our 95% probability on the road to accountability.

The Accountability Advantage

Let's face it, most of us will do pretty much anything to achieve our goals.

While self-motivation is vital, extra motivation, support, assistance and sage advice from an Accountability Partner will act as a catalyst for reaching your goals. The catalytic reaction to positive reinforcement from an Accountability Partner is truly beneficial, and should never be taken for granted.

It is important, however, how you choose your Accountability Partner. Before you consider this, you should look at the following criteria. Your Accountability Partner should be:

☑ **Someone who's been there before.** This is someone who you can look up to and respect. Someone who has already achieved what you want to achieve. As I like to say, they 'walk the talk' and have successfully traversed the path already, which is a similar path you are looking to travel. The path need not be exactly the same.

Having a university degree, similar industry or business experience is in my opinion NOT essential.

Certainly, you want someone who has a successful track record themselves of entrepreneurial success and yes, even failures can mean they typically would have a playbook that is filled with strategy, advice and useful tips which are underpinned by an arsenal of experience that your business can surely benefit from.

☑ **Someone not emotionally connected to your world.** You need to find a person who comes across with a neutral approach to helping you – this is why choosing a friend, family member, or a close acquaintance DOES NOT work well, and it always ends uncomfortably. Largely because there is already an emotional connection underpinning your relationship at the moment, so this means they almost always cannot have those difficult and hard questions with you when it's needed. It's counterintuitive to your existing relationship and it's really hard to separate your private relationship from the business relationship. After all business is business, where clear thinking is required. Any conflict of interest, and protecting feelings causes more damage and it inhibits your leadership capability and strategy implementation and execution. Don't do it, it's not worth the hassle and wasted energy.

☑ **A person who understands that failure is normal.** This may seem a little weird, but you are not judged by the number of times you succeed, but rather, by the number of times you fail and keep trying. Remember Mr Turnbull from our earlier chapter? Mr Turnbull said that to me back in the 1980s, and it's still appropriate and relevant today.

As I see it, if you don't fail at some time during your entrepreneurial journey, then I'd be questioning whether or not you are truly pushing yourself hard enough. I say you are not stretching yourself high, big or wide enough.

If you are NOT biting off a massive goal or task, and learning how to sort it out on the fly, getting it done by chewing like hell, then ask yourself, are the goals you are setting high enough?

Do you set goals which force you to stretch? If not, then you need set tougher ones. C'mon, it's time to be honest with yourself, otherwise who are you really impressing?

☑ **Someone relatable, and who makes you feel safe.** It's key that you and your Accountability Partner have a chemistry that enables you to work together. Deciding whether or not they are the right fit for you and whether you'd like to engage them for you and your business, getting a clear understanding of skill sets, experience and how they will handle situations will give you a clear sense of temperament, energy levels and drive. After all, ensuring you connect is vital – chemistry is important.

Feeling that you are in safe hands is key. Trust is really critical for you to both speak frankly, honestly and critically. Feeling safe in this situation encourages open discussion, which is how you will get the best from each other.

☑ **Someone professional.** Professionalism is critical to ensure both parties do not waste valuable time and get things done efficiently. At the commencement of your program with your Accountability Partner you should sign a formal Rules of Engagement (Service Agreement) that covers each party's responsibilities and how the program works.

In this document, should also include a Non-Disclosure Agreement for both parties (your Accountability Partner and you) to sign. Check your Accountability Partner's references, call the clients directly to find out more and ask about the experience and outcomes achieved, and talk about temperament and chemistry.

I've seen many people try unsuccessfully to partner with others such as friends and family members, all to no avail. Often the process is a waste of time, which costs you money and reputation. In fact, I've gained clients who wished to engage me privately to work with them one-on-one as a result of previous failed past Accountability Partner relationships with others.

Danger, danger, danger – beware of appointing your Life Partner and/or Business Partner to be your Accountability Partner. This is danger, danger, danger. While the intention is genuine and it's coming from the right place, the execution doesn't work because of sensitivities surrounding the fact that you are too close to each other, too emotionally connected and typically unable to engage in truly honest and sometimes (always) challenging conversations about you personally which can be hurtful. Perhaps you are not meeting your obligations, you are not hitting your goals, you regularly let others down because you are not keeping the promises you make to others, and most importantly the promises you have given to yourself. Maybe your business partner and you are not working together as a cohesive team; perhaps you are just not in sync and you need to dig deep to understand and address this. It's hard to discuss those important elements freely, truthfully and honestly under these circumstances. The result is you will be pissing off those people around you who are important to you, those people who are close to you, those people who care about and love you.

Avoiding this is crucial for building successful companies. Be careful and choose your Accountability Partner wisely.

Once you're happy with your Accountability Partner, you would need to create your agreed 'ways of work'. This is a formal schedule or framework, to ensure that the process is taken seriously.

The agreement should outline your agreed **protocols**; the accepted or established code of procedure or behaviour in any group, organisation or situation.

Your protocols should include:

☑ **Ways of work.** This should include: the date and time when you will meet up (it's important to have a regular set time that you both know in advance and it's diarised, so no excuses).

   Discuss how you will communicate (SMS, email, face to face, Zoom, etc.), the location where you will meet, etc.

☑ **Mutual expectations.** A written set of expectations between the Accountability Partner and yourself as the recipient.

☑ **A feedback system.** Deciding how you will provide each other feedback on what is working versus what is not working.

☑ **An understanding of personalities.** Your Accountability Partner needs to understand how you operate as a person – what motivates you, what scares you, and what hurts you. Knowing more about you will better equip your partner to guide, push and pull where necessary and appropriate to hold you to account.

Committing to your Accountability Partner and being set on meeting at least once a month is a start ... Personally, I prefer to talk weekly to check in with my clients. It gives me an opportunity to provide advice, counsel, support, clarity, encouragement and celebration. Then we'll have a longer session with more formal outcomes and robust discussion once every month.

Every session – both the Weekly Check-In and my Monthly Catch Up – is followed up with Session Notes and Action Items, so there are NO excuses for non-completion and lack of understanding. Not knowing and/or forgetting to do something can no longer be used as an excuse. It's worked a treat for my clients ... why not give it a go?

You must set meetings in your calendar, and using applications such as Outlook, Google or Apple Calendars works really well as you can send invitations to lock in future sessions. It is ideal if you are using Zoom, Skype or FaceTime to connect with your Accountability Partner, then you can include the links and a password, if required.

One of the things you may need to do differently is to broadcast your goals to the world!

Why you should share your goals with family, friends, and your YES Accountability Partner

I say ... tell *everyone*, and tell them loudly. There's a method behind the madness.

There are compelling reasons why you SHOULD tell the entire world about your goals, plans and dreams.

I get that it is not always a simple process for everyone to share their goals, because there may be some that are rather personal. In addition, there may be some fears of failure that arise from sharing your goals with others. Fears like, *what happens if I don't achieve them?*

However, sharing your goals is an immensely liberating process. For me, I've often found that by sharing you create a network of people around you; your inner circle – call it coming together as your team, ready to support, counsel and celebrate with you as you achieve your goals.

People who share their goals will be broadcasting it to their family, friends, colleagues and anyone else that makes sense. Some of your goals may be aided by these people that you share your success with.

When I share my experience in writing books, I always think about **accountability** and the power it generates.

Let's go back to 2012, when I embarked on my author journey for the very first time. At this time, I was in the marine and lifestyle industry, a Cofounder and Dealer Principal of St Kilda Boat Sales and Service Centre, located at St Kilda Marina and at Wyndham Harbour in Melbourne.

The opportunity that writing offers you to position yourself as a specialist in your area and a thought leader in your field is truly enormous and its power cannot ever be overstated. After sitting in a class with 45 other entrepreneurs and listening to Andrew Griffiths talk about the benefits of self-publishing a book, it gave me a 'light bulb moment' as I realised with great excitement that I could write a book to use as a sales tool to better position myself as an expert in my industry ... which would in turn position my business as the 'go-to place' for boating needs. I was caught, hook, line and sinker.

I quickly made a decision to write a book on boating, which was much needed in the marketplace, and it would be called *Honey, let's buy a BOAT!*

Boat buyers, my potential clients, did not know how to safely buy a boat, and what was the preferred process to follow to ensure they got the right boat and the right price. The central question perfectly suited me and my business; this was authentically in my wheelhouse as they say. It aligned to my WHY and my purpose.

Over the next 200 days, every day and every night, when I had free time, I would madly and obsessively write my manuscript, ensuring I got all of my boating experiences and knowledge onto paper. About 10 weeks into my writing process was my 50th birthday, and my wonderful wife Suzi organised a big party, together with our sons, Jeremy and Adam.

There were 150 people in attendance: my mum and dad were there, both my in-laws, family and friends, ... it was a wonderful night, one to truly remember. Suzi and my boys gave a lovely speech about our wonderful lives together, my mates – bless them – they gave me one hell of a roasting, complete with pranks at my expense. It was wonderful to share this moment with those who are important to me, and it is safe to say that I was an emotional wreck, tears flowed from my eyes and all that was important to me was there, in one room to celebrate this milestone.

The momentum of the evening changed somewhat when during my speech – much to everyone's surprise – I told the gathering that I was ... drum roll please ... in the process of writing a book ...

'What the f#$%' was heard really clearly coming from a large number of people in the room.

I said in a big and proud voice the book was to be called *Honey, let's buy a BOAT!* and it would be finished and ready for production in about 120 days, which I told everyone confidently just in time for the start of the coming summer boating season which was 1 October 2012.

Wow, what a shock to the audience ... Adam, my youngest son, shouted out, 'but dad you don't even read books, so how will you write one?' He was honest and this was actually correct, I thought to myself, but of course I would never admit it. This was followed by another truth from my eldest son Jeremy – he yelled 'how can you write a book ... you failed English at school, then you got expelled dad,' or are you 'too old to remember'. Boy, was I copping a basting!

This announcement was definitely NOT the result of too much alcohol, otherwise known as truth serum at my own party. However, behind my apparent madness was a genuine method, and pure genius as I reflect.

Taking a leaf from Steve Jobs, looking back at those major public announcements made by Apple were then, and are now, significant events in the history of Apple. I've always found that one of the BEST ways to hold yourself (and your teams) to account and thereby making yourself truly accountable to others, is to make BIG announcements and share stuff with others. Stuff like goals, targets, wins, loses, success and failure should be shared with others and not be the world's best kept secret. Make your announcement loud and clear so your intention and that of your team is known by everyone. Formulate it in advance ... be prepared.

Here's the thing; I knew that everyone listening, all 150, would remember that announcement, and remember that night forever, or till at least I had finished writing my manuscript, which was long enough to suit my purposes.

This is one of my fundamentals of accountability. You've got to tell others about your intentions.

The more people that know the better – telling everyone is perfect. It is so simple and easy to do, yet it's guaranteed to get you results. Everyone who hears your intentions will want to regularly check in on your progress, giving you support, providing counsel and, if needed, they will give you a precise bum kicking and, yes, we all need that at times when we fall behind.

They will also celebrate your success with you, genuinely proud and thrilled to bits with your achievements. As my dear family and friends did after my 50th: they were calling me regularly to check on my writing progress. They were sending me texts; my friends accepted the reason why I was cancelling social arrangements to allow me more time to write. They got it;

they totally understood how important it was to me to achieve my goal. Their involvement, their loving support, knowledge and appreciation of the gravitas of what I was doing was the best way to ensure that I was going to meet my deadline and achieve my goals on time.

You see, I was never going to let down 150 people very close to me, and I wasn't going to let myself down as a result. What a remarkable outcome and process that was. 'Tell the world' works incredibly well.

Naturally, my book was written on time and before my due date by 72 hours. That book is still being sold today, it was #5 on the iTunes bookstore as a bestseller and won a boating industry award. Another goal was achieved, and another box ticked. Right now, I'm writing my fourth book and I've repeated that exact process over and over again, and it works.

Tell the world of your intentions, so those around you can rally to help you to be fully accountable.

A goal without a plan is just a wish.

Did you know ...

- ☑ Setting small goals allows for more frequent wins. That's a great feeling.
- ☑ Reaching these goals keeps you motivated. We all need a purpose.
- ☑ Staying motivated helps you crush more goals. Play your best game.

> **'Success on any major scale requires you to accept responsibility ... In the final analysis, the one quality that all successful people have is the ability to take on responsibility.'**
> *Michael Korda*

Knowing when to share your goals

There's a time to share your goals, and it may not always be on the day that you set them or at your 50th birthday party, like it was for me. It could even be two or three months into it, maybe it could be within the first minute that you set the goal.

Whenever it is, you would need to assess for yourself based on the following criteria:

☑ If it's a goal that you have been procrastinating on for a while, or if you have a goal that has been dormant for a long time, as soon as you mention it in public, you'll have external accountability from everyone, and people will be asking you continuously about how you're coming along in achieving that goal – which may annoy and frustrate some who are struggling to complete it.

☑ Is it a goal that you need your network to know of? These are goals where you know that by sharing it, your network will reach out to you with assistance or guidance on achieving that goal. It could also be a goal that you want others to join you in on – such as losing weight or practising mindfulness together, or even reducing your business expenses or achieving that sales target.

☑ Is it a competitive goal? If part of your goal involves entering competitions, then it would be valuable to share that goal with people a few months before the competition. In that way, you will gain momentum and external support to catapult your habits into action.

What could possibly stop you from sharing your goals?

You may not want to tell anyone about your goals or plans because you don't want anyone to know if you fail in your attempt.

Have you ever been so afraid of failing at something that you decided not to give it a try in the first place? I have, and that is a horrible feeling. Mr Turnbull knew that I was not ready to jump back on the horse after I'd fallen off pretty heavily. But he knew the importance for me of jumping back in the saddle and trying again.

Or has a fear of failure led you to subconsciously undermine your efforts to avoid the possibility of more significant failure, so you didn't get back in the saddle?

Fear of failure can be paralysing, leaving you numb with fear, and leading you to procrastination and a lack of self-belief – so you do nothing. You know that if we allow fear to hold back our progress in life, we are likely to miss some significant opportunities along the way. Accountability creates activity, activity creates opportunity and opportunity is where I've always made money.

An experience might have been so terrible and left you with such scars that you became afraid of failing in other aspects. Scared that history will repeat.

Past problems can be associated with many causes. Whatever has stopped you from achieving things in the past may still be present. The monkey is still on your back, and you don't have a plan to deal with it – while hoping it will go away, you also know it won't.

Solutions:

- ☑ Things don't disappear on their own. You need to make the commitment to 'let it go'. If you don't make this conscious choice up front, you could also end up self-sabotaging any effort to move on from this past hurt.

- ☑ In every moment you have that choice – to continue to feel bad about history or to *start feeling good*. You need to *take responsibility* for your own happiness, and not put such power into the hands of a past event.

- ☑ Now it's time to let go. Let go of the past, and stop reliving it. Furthermore, stop telling yourself you can't do this. You can't undo the past, all you can do is to make today the best day of your life.

No one cares: no Accountability Partner, no Coach and no Buddy

If you don't have anyone to hold YOU accountable, and a deadline passes without any fuss, it's like no one cares. Yet if you shared the completion date with someone else, they would be checking in with your progress, assisting you to work through the awkward moments, and helping you get across that finish line to meet your date and time commitment.

Despite what you may think, you just can't do it alone. There is little glory in a solo failure, so swallow that pride and ask for some help, advice, or clarity. Sure, you might have to return the favour someday, but that's what colleagues are for – they can make great Accountability Buddies.

Remember, you have to live outside your comfort zone to achieve anything new. Sharing your goals with others will, without a doubt, be uncomfortable and make you feel vulnerable – but that is where your growth lies!

Let me introduce you to Anoushka Gungadin

I have recorded a Zoom session with Anoushka, who is a Future of Work, Cultural Intelligence and Inclusive Leadership specialist with a keen interest in emerging economies. Key focus areas of her work include: stakeholder engagement, corporate affairs, bilateral trade, health-tech.

Anoushka's full bio appears below.

Bonus video

Watch, the video recording of my full interview with Anoushka conducted over Zoom; due to COVID restrictions and stage-4 isolation at the time of recording, on my website. Please visit www.tickthoseboxes.com.au/TheAccountabilityAdvantage

Here's my discussion with Anoushka.

DARREN: Anoushka, you are the CEO of the ANZ India Chamber of Commerce. You're a speaker and future work and inclusive leadership specialist. I know that you've been a former CEO of the Duke of Edinburgh's Award in Victoria, and that you have lived and worked across multiple continents: India, Africa, Europe.

So, tell me, what are your experiences with the term 'accountability'? What does that mean to you?

ANOUSHKA: Accountability is a big part of my life. Obviously, wearing multiple hats, as you see at the moment with the Chamber of Commerce, running my own consulting, my role on the boards; accountability really for me is that crucial part of being able to do those as well managing my life. As a mum, I've got two children who are in primary school, and having some time for myself to keep fit. I think for me accountability is part of my support network, part of making me achieve what I set out to do.

DARREN: Yes, so you had to rebuild your strategy for this year. Talk to me about prioritising. Is it the same principal prioritising for the 10 and 11 year olds at home as it is with your teams in a commercial sense?

ANOUSHKA: I think the similarity is where we have this shared code of conduct. We said we were going to work at this time and talk at that time, so I think that's shared. With the team as well, we need to know the dates that we hold our meetings, we need to know how we can give feedback, we need to know how we can lean into each other and create that safe space. So, I think from that big-picture point of view it is similar, but then how I engage the execution of that with the kids as opposed to my team would be different.

DARREN: Of course. Do you feel that the word 'consequences', perhaps even the word 'penalty', comes into discussion in accountability conversations?

ANOUSHKA: You know, those words have very a negative connotation for many people. But at the same time, if you do something, whether you like it or not there are consequences. For me, I have responsibility in anything I am part of. Taking responsibility for what didn't work out gives me that power, so if I blame someone else, if I've put that into someone else's hands I can't do anything about it. I guess as a coach as well, when I work with clients it is a power tool that I share around blame or responsibility, being the two ends of that spectrum.

So, there are consequences, there are penalties whether you like it or not. I wouldn't shy away from it. And if you have that in mind then you can also assess the risk and that doubt. You know, not everything works out well. I mean, we are human, we will make mistakes. But how we do act when we make mistakes is crucial.

DARREN: Absolutely. What's the best method you found in dealing with either your coaching clients or perhaps even your management teams of getting them to take responsibility and match that to an outcome?

ANOUSHKA: I think sharing and communicating from the very beginning. I am quite a big-picture person; I can work with very little information; so, for me my challenge is to recognise that some people in my team need all the information and maybe more than once. So, for me it's also recognising that people need different things. So, making sure I'm giving enough information; sometimes you can't give out everything, sometimes I don't know everything; and being okay to not know as well, and supporting the team. You can't say 'this is what we need to do', and then disappear; and then the event happens and there are mistakes. Where was I throughout that whole process?

So, I love to grow people. Of course, there is a bit of a challenge. But at the same time, I do create a space for support. And there should be ways where someone can come and say, 'I really am stuck here, I can't do this, so how do we deal with this together?' You know, having your team's back is a culture that you need to create, it doesn't happen overnight. So, for me that's very important.

The Anoushka Gungadin Story

Anoushka is an experienced CEO, Board Director, International Speaker and Certified Coach, with a 20-year career across Australia, Asia, Europe and Africa.

A connector of people, culture and opportunities, she is passionate about inclusive leadership, future of work and emerging economies.

She is the CEO of the Australia India Chamber of Commerce; founder of GlobalCQ, an award-winning organisation that connects employers to diverse talent; Director of the health-tech business Allevi8; and Director of the Fin-tech group Anglo African Investments.

Anoushka heads TiE Women in Australia, a global network that supports and funds women-led businesses.

Anoushka is the former CEO of The Duke of Edinburgh's Award Australia-Vic, preceded by more than 10 years heading finance for an international French law firm in China. Her past experience includes working with UNESCO, Mondelēz and L'Oréal.

'If you are building a culture where honest expectations are communicated and peer accountability is the norm, then the group will address poor performance and attitudes.'
Henry Cloud

Chapter 6

Find a person to hold you to account

Moves you to 95% – if you have a specific accountability appointment with a person you've committed to.

95%

The Road to Accountability

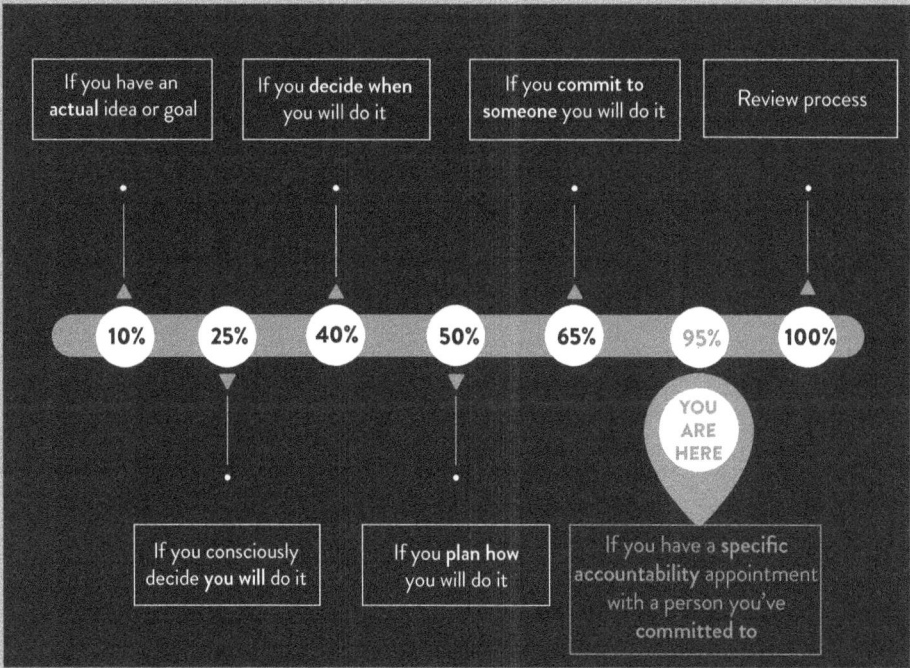

| If you have an **actual** idea or goal | If you **decide when** you will do it | If you **commit to someone** you will do it | Review process |

10% — 25% — 40% — 50% — 65% — 95% — 100%

| If you consciously decide **you will** do it | If you **plan how** you will do it | If you have a **specific accountability** appointment with a person you've **committed to** |

YOU ARE HERE

Based on the 2010 study conducted by the American Society of Training and Development (ASTD).

On our road to accountability '*if you have a specific accountability appointment with a person you've committed to*', your probability soars to a **massive 95%**. Fantastic stuff … you are nearly there.

This is where an Accountability Partner comes to the fore, by providing you with specific feedback and support to get you over the line and track your goals alongside your plan and priorities to ensure you stay the course without diversion.

In this chapter we'll cover four key components:

- ☑ The true meaning of accountability.

- ☑ How to make accountability a habit.

- ☑ How to find an Accountability Partner.

- ☑ Group Accountability Forums.

An Accountability Partner is a secret weapon that drives you forward. It allows you to set bigger goals than you would normally set, and to achieve them. The beauty of finding someone to hold you accountable is that when it's done precisely, you see the results in a short time, and you get to quickly taste the success that drives you on and moves you forward.

At that exact moment, for the first time in perhaps a long time, you have an incredible opportunity to eradicate overwork, overcome fear, become clear about your goals and actually achieve them. In a few days, you will have stopped going around in circles and start executing like the person you wanted to be. In just weeks from now, as more of your goals get knocked over, you'll uncover new opportunities that would have stayed hidden for years, or perhaps forever. You'll turn vague dreams into bite-sized action plans that get completed, without excuses, blame, finger pointing or distraction.

As the months go by, you will manage larger, bolder projects with ease, and finally be at the top of your business, rather than holed up beneath it. Along with this comes having that dreaded 'to-do list' begging for mercy. Best of all? You will stop feeling overwhelmed, overworked, lost and trapped, and start to comprehend your business growth with crystal-clear clarity and unstoppable confidence. All this can happen faster than you think.

On average, my clients witness positive changes in their productivity and work–life balance within a few weeks of our sessions commencing. My initial Unboxing Session gives them immediate relief and increased clarity of what needs to be done, when it's needed, and a picture of what lies ahead in the pursuit of their goals.

You'll need to set a plan of what needs to be achieved, and there's NO reason at all why you can't become an even higher achiever too. By making good on those promises you made to yourself and to those who depend on you daily. Others who are currently being let down and are quite possibly pissed off, as your promises and goals are not being actively pursued with that laser focus we talked about earlier.

I know some of you might be saying, 'nope, this won't work'. I can understand why you may say that. After all, for so many of you there have been plenty of other purposeful programs and big promises made to you from others which have fallen short. My experience tells me that this is because they don't focus on how you can implement and execute in a timely fashion. There's no one to work with you hands on, to roll up their sleeves and get down and dirty with you with regularity, which is needed and mission critical for YOU to stay on track and to not lose interest or be distracted from the goals set. Others can talk at a high level with a big-picture view, but as we all know it's the 'taking action' that makes all the difference between you achieving your goals and not.

Perhaps along your journey there have been other coaches who have failed to uncover your full potential by creating events and programs focusing on a wonderful new strategy and renewed business focus, which gave you a superficial experience. That was a quick and short-lived buzz for you and your business, but nothing has changed. You know the ones who paint a glossy big-picture vision for what your new world looks like, and they make it look pretty darn good. This gives you a hormone release, and with that comes a renewed sense of hope and expectation, that all is not lost ...

It's a sublime feeling of being pumped and high on energy. It's even nice to get caught up in the flashing lights and loud music for a time, escaping the true reality of your world. Perhaps it gives you a huge kick-butt 'big hairy audacious goal' which seems fantastic at the time, but all that soon wore off and was quickly forgotten when the reality of your honest existence hit home. You cannot just band-aid or window dress this stuff. It's deep within you, and it requires you to find a different strategy, another route to your location.

Your return from the world of make believe becomes apparent when you're working alone; by yourself as you do daily. Especially today, when you are dealing with the daily struggle of your company. There are issues, problems as people challenge you, which mount up. Your best-thought-out plan to attack these wonderfully liberating new strategies goes out the window really quickly when you realise you are alone and it's the same, same.

You feel totally overwhelmed by the sheer volume of what you *must do*, as you compare that with all that you *can do*. It seems that all the beating of your chest and walking on hot coals has long since been diluted by the reality and seriousness of your situation.

Right now, your reality is that you are most likely juggling too many balls at once, trying desperately not to drop any of them. Have I got that right?

If so, that's one of the clues as to why you need a specific person to hold you accountable.

Imagine if ... you could have someone who actually cares about you, who is on your team. Someone who is in your corner, all of the time. Not a friend, nor a life partner, who both have an emotional connection with you, making it hard to say what they really mean so as to not hurt feelings and to protect the ones they love. But rather from someone at arm's length, who provides you a viewpoint from an outsider looking in and seeing the entire picture for what it is. No sugar coating here. No responding 'that's awesome' just to make you feel good. Here, there is no emotional connection, which mandates uncomfortable barriers to show support and encouragement. But rather, giving you honest, straight-up, strong advice and feedback. You'll get plenty of counsel, advice and tips based upon their own entrepreneurial journey of having 'waked the talk' and travelling along the same road to accountability that you are now navigating. They will have done so, many times over, with success to back it up.

In addition, they will celebrate with you when you tick those boxes and hit your goals and set the next goal with a stretch, so you extend yourself and grow in stature, self-confidence and as a leader. Along with celebrations comes the inevitable kick in the butt when you need it. *You will, and you know that.*

Let's face it, we all need that kick along from time to time on our business journey. Those uncomfortable moments along with those awkward times are important for your growth and the honing of your business skills. It's these moments which force you and your coach to have those *tough* and *awkward conversations* which are often needed to pick you up, to realign your priorities and to reset your focus and energy. Importantly, your Accountability Coach, Partner or Buddy will be your sounding block for challenging times, now that you are no longer alone and feeling isolated. Immediately, this changes everything. You will feel be very well supported in all of your endeavours by your Accountability Coach, Partner or Buddy.

Business and life are unpredictable, so you'll be blessed that your Accountability Coach, Partner or Buddy is dependable. You can rely on them (and their team) to be in your corner for your journey. They should do it precisely, and will check in with you at set times each and every week to make this a ritual and to ensure that you are heading down the right track by hitting the milestones and goals along your road to accountability. In doing this, you are building good habits and a solid work ethic, which is underpinned by frequency. We know that frequency and regularity are key to building good habits and ensuring your continuity of plan and clarity of message. These positive actions will influence you to implement and execute your priority and focus so you are ready to meet those deadlines and commitments. The execution of which will ensure you reach 95% probability of achieving your goals, tasks and projects.

With my ongoing and continued success in this field I've become known as *The Accountability Guy*® and I cannot afford to risk my reputation by making promises that I cannot deliver on, or doing anything short of getting incredible results for the people I work with. It's this philosophy that's allowed me to achieve a 97.8 client satisfaction score over a recent 12-month period. This is underwritten by countless numbers of glowing reviews and tangible results from businesses all across the globe. Perhaps most important of all, my systems are robust and formed using proven principles within the road to accountability frameworks and strategies. The end result is that I help business owners and executives become truly accountable, and grow in all kinds of new ways, beyond monetary, which is a given.

In fact, the only way my frameworks will not work, is if *you* do not to apply them correctly and in a timely fashion, which an outstanding Accountability Partner, Coach or Buddy will make sure YOU DO!

Call me biased, but here's why I believe an expert Accountability Partner, Coach or Buddy to be the best investment you'll make in your business.

There are many things you can buy for your business – new cars, new computers, new desks, even new people. But without rock-solid accountability in place, you're building a brick house on quicksand. Time and time again, I've seen great businesses, brilliant products, superior services, and hard-working, intelligent people fall from grace as their business consumes them, and they slowly stagnate and die a slow death which consumes and drowns many good people.

Investing in proven systems that will hold you and your team accountable is, therefore, an intelligent and profitable investment for hundreds of CEOs, business owners and their teams.

You can't afford to wait

Without the ability to set goals and achieve them, each day is another missed opportunity and another setback on your journey to play your best game.

Invest now in the road to accountability and engage a specific Accountability Partner, Coach or Buddy while it's fresh in your mind and you're motivated to finally do something about your situation. Take action. Remember what Keith Abraham CSP said: 'The day you take the first step of the task you have been procrastinating about – the task that may be holding you back – is the day you beat procrastination!'

How to find an Accountability Partner, Coach or Buddy

> **'Intentions do not insulate us from the consequences of our actions.'**
> *Jon D Harrison*

Congratulations, so you have finally decided to share your accountability journey with an Accountability Partner, Coach or Buddy. That's a prudent decision which you won't regret.

Now it's time to decide WHO that person will be, and HOW your Accountability Partner, Coach or Buddy will be involved in your journey.

This brings us to the climax of my book. Remember earlier, we removed the idea of having your life partner, family member or friend be your Accountability Partner, Coach or Buddy, so now we need to go outside your inner circle and recruit the right person.

Let's begin with some much-needed clarification and a definition of an Accountability Partner, Coach or Buddy, so there is no confusion.

An **Accountability Partner** or **Buddy** is a non-paid role whereby you both take on that role for each other, and you hopefully both will equally benefit.

On the other hand, an **Accountability Coach**, in direct contrast, is a professional, a person who is remunerated (paid for services or work performed) and whose entire task and goal is to keep you on track, and provide the guidance and motivation necessary so you can achieve your goals within set deadlines. Their goal is for you to achieve your goals.

An Accountability Coach also provides assistance in laying out a clear plan, breaking it down into smaller objectives and prioritising them with respect to urgency and importance, aligned to your WHY and purpose.

Apart from that, an Accountability Coach will keep regular tabs on you to ensure you're meeting your own expectations and achieving those goals. Along the way, they will give you the appreciation that motivates and comforts you when things don't go as you would like. They are your professional guardian who guides you along the path of success and sticks with you in both good and bad times.

To find the RIGHT person, look for someone who has a proven track record of being able to get things done themselves. Forget the university degrees; while that is nice to have, it doesn't always mean they have successfully 'walked the talk' and have a proven track record. Against popular belief, they DO NOT NEED to have been working in the same sector or industry as you are in. In fact, the broader the experience they have, the better find they will be. They can bring a fresh perspective.

It can be hard to find the right person, but you must no matter how long it takes. Here are some specific activities and suggestions of where you may find what you are looking for.

Networking events

One of the places you could find an Accountability Partner, Coach or Buddy is by attending conferences, BNI meetings, TEDx evenings, association or networking events. My experience is that these attendees are typically a collection of people who are goal-driven, like-minded people, all with some interest in personal and professional development.

It is likely that you will find a mix of people at these types of events, and will likely find someone who has the qualities you desire. Take a moment to introduce yourself and exchange contact details to explore the possibilities of an accountability partnership and see what direction it heads. Consider it like a job interview for a new hire.

LinkedIn

LinkedIn is a hub of resources for someone looking to find an Accountability Partner, Coach or Buddy.

You're able to scour and search the entire database for someone. Use it wisely, and don't just 'spam' everyone that you know. Consider each contact's network, look at their profile, and their career path. Read the articles they wrote. Then make a formal and personal introduction when you send them an invite. The idea is to move the conversation from LinkedIn to an offline relationship, and discuss the mutual benefits of accountability.

Leverage your network

Ask for an introduction – this is where the part of 'sharing your goals' comes in.

If you share your goals with your network, then you're able to leverage off them. Perhaps someone who has seen your goals knows an influential person in your field. Use this as an opportunity to get in contact with that person and make use of your network to achieve your goals.

Pick me, pick me

Okay, time to pump up my tyres, so skip ahead if you prefer not to listen to my unsolicited plug.

I say forget about the hassle and awkwardness of having to search for an Accountability Partner, and why reinvent the wheel? Simply use my expertise and experience – you can engage me to work with you privately in one my One-On-One programs held over six months or twelve months.

Alternatively, I've got my 'Group Accountability Forum' (Mastermind) Program, where you organise a small group of between 3 and 7 of your alumni, colleagues or cohort together, and I'll facilitate your accountability meetings personally.

To learn more about my accountability programs visit: www.tickthoseboxes.com.au/working-with-me/

Gift a copy of this book

If you like what I'm talking about, it's a wonderful idea to **gift** to a family member, friend or colleague **a copy of this book** so they too understand the road to accountability, and the success which can be found at your destination.

BONUS OFFER: If you think a gift of this book is a good idea for a family member, friend or colleague, then send me an email to df@tickthoseboxes.com.au and tell me that you wish to gift a copy and I'll email you a *secret discount code* that will SAVE you a few bucks on your purchase as a token of my sincere appreciation.

Accountability Groups (Forums or Masterminds)

You might be wondering if you can bring together a group of like-minded businesspeople to form an Accountability Group, and would that work and what might it look like? The answer is yes, absolutely you can.

I call them a Group Accountability Forum, and they work well. In fact, I was part of a fantastic group of individuals, and we worked together for over four years, making significant inroads into our goals and business ideas by sharing knowledge and peer-to-peer accountability.

The group consisted of entrepreneurs, which is how we were brought together in the first instance, from various different industries and sectors. We had an Innovation Consultant, Corporate Heath/Personal Trainer, Lawyer, Financial Planner, Event Management, Architect and me – I was in the Marine and Lifestyle industry at the time, on my own entrepreneurial journey. All seven of us worked beautifully together as a cohesive team.

It's with this knowledge and my personal experiences in dealing with Group Accountability that I write this section to answer common questions.

What is an Accountability Group?

An Accountability Group is a small group of, ideally, three to seven persons. Based on experience, I'm really quite fixed on this number because any more than seven and it's too hard to ensure everyone has equal time during your sessions. With this number of people each session should run for a maximum of two hours or so. Any more people and it's too hard to manage the all-important follow-ups and regular communications outside your session times. Any less and you lose the shared knowledge benefits of a gathering of like-minded people from different industries. You also don't want the additional worry and concern of whether or not you have good numbers of attendees to make a quorum. Otherwise, you may as well engage in your own one-on-one session privately with your own coach.

For group sessions to work effectively, all Accountability Groups members must share their work in a totally open and honest manner; secrets are not allowed. More about your group's rules and requirements, which I call 'protocols', later.

The advantages of Accountability Groups

The main advantage is that as a group you will help each other to stay motivated along your journey. Shared learning is wonderful as you all work to support and assist each other's endeavours, plans and goals. Having others hold you responsible for the work you do on a daily, weekly, monthly, quarterly and yearly basis is a fantastic way to swing your bottom into action.

Being social creatures as we are, we respond well to being around and associated with others, especially with those who you like or want to be like. We've all got people who inspire us and who we'd like to be more like, and we long to receive praise and recognition for the work we do. This is why Accountability Groups have worked for me, and why they were so successful for my fellow group members too.

What a great way to network, to learn from others' experiences, and for peer-to-peer accountability to ensure you are on track working towards your goals. It's also a wonderful opportunity to expand your network of connections, to broaden your horizons and to see what other people are working on, and how they go about achieving their own goals. The shared-learning, peer-to-peer accountability and connectivity are the components that I've always found really interesting indeed, and something I learn so much from and continue to do so.

I love learning from what others are doing, understanding what's important, what their priorities are – this is all so incredibly valuable, and will save you and your business valuable time, and much energy, and learning from others is a proven way to save you money and it can reduce stress.

Sharing the 'what works' and 'what does not' is a valuable exercise indeed. So too is the direct group and peer-to-peer accountability aspect, which comes from not letting yourself down, and dare I say it, embarrassing yourself with others you admire and respect. Allowing yourself to perform in the presence of others, and embracing open and honest discussion, for me was simply wonderful. Engaging in strong debate, being able to provide meaningful and specific feedback to others and for me to receive it in return was priceless, which I know saved me real and measurable $$$ in the long term. This was because I could make important decisions for my business as I would receive meaningful, well-chosen and well-intentioned criticism and analysis from like-minded and successful business folks with whom I totally respected. This for me, this was a very healthy outcome and good for business. In fact, these same people today form part of my inner circle of go-to people that I respect, trust and admire.

Tips for creating a successful Accountability Group

If you are looking to establish an Accountability Group, it's important to consider what you are hoping to achieve from the collective support the group can provide. Once you have that in mind, you can then search for like-minded individuals who might be interested in joining. It might be tempting to just stick to close friends, but you know why we should stay right away from that, and try to reach out to others you might usually not associate with.

Working with family and friends to provide accountability, as we've already discussed, is bad business practice as you might be more tempted to 'let each other off the hook' or to find yourselves chatting away rather than being productive.

Don't be disheartened if you find an Accountability Group and it isn't for you. Not everyone will respond to it, and you might find it isn't right for you, so finding and engaging an Accountability Coach to work with you in private sessions may be better suited to your personality. More confident and outgoing people will find it easier than those who are shy and a little anxious.

> **'The only way we succeed as a group is not simply following directions, but in keeping each other accountable for our actions.'**
> J. Darkholme

If you are considering creating a group, another important consideration is the location. If you are all from different locations then online sessions work an absolute treat. Look at using Facebook groups to connect, use an online messaging system like WhatsApp to manage your group, and communication is easy and cheap. Skype, Google Meet and Zoom can all connect everyone, and chat rooms, breakout rooms and whiteboards come in handy. Since the pandemic we've all become very familiar with online meetings, so you are probably already familiar with how to do this. The ability to record your virtual sessions for later reflection, review and to provide clarity is a MUST. Weekly voice calls or WhatsApp messages can be scheduled to see where everyone is up to. For those fortunate to live in close proximity and COVID permitting, you could do this face to face. Nothing beats you all being together in one room, eyeballing each other and reading body language. Finding suitable space is easy: simply rotate amongst your group members (who have meeting rooms to use) or rent a meeting room from your local co-working space; alternatively, you can book a private room at a restaurant – having a meal together after the session is a fun idea. Libraries can also have rooms you can use.

For those people wanting to try Group Accountability, may I suggest you now read *'My Group Accountability Protocols'* which are key to ensure clarity, understanding, and a good work ethic within your group. To download your FREE copy from my website, please visit: www.tickthoseboxes.com.au/free-stuff/

My 'protocols' are commercially prudent for all past and present Group Accountability Forum and Mastermind participants. These protocols, which each member will read and sign their acceptance, ensure members play nicely with each other, and are your group's Rules and Conditions which every attendee agrees to, and they govern each participant, both past and present, and your sessions. The protocols confirm that members are committed to attend each forum session, and they will remain open and honest with feedback. Most importantly, they are respectful to each other. I suggest you and your newly formed group create your own protocols, which each member will sign off and accept *prior to* your first session. Each member signing makes a commitment to accept the group's rules of engagement. Should anyone be unwilling to sign, then ask them to move on, as your values and focus are not aligned.

If arranging your group sounds like it's too hard, I'll gladly offer to facilitate and chair your Group Accountability Forum each meeting. Either face to face if you're in Melbourne, otherwise we'll use Zoom, which is my personal preference.

I'll work closely with your main organiser to set up your group and will provide Action Items and circulate to members (like minutes at a meeting), and follow up prior to each session. It's great to leave all this in my safe hands, adding a whole new layer of accountability to your group sessions, so you can focus on the needs of your business, rather than logistics, facilitation and reporting requirements. To find out more about my Group Accountability Forum (Mastermind), please visit: www.tickthoseboxes.com.au/working-with-me/

Timing is everything – right now you need to create that plan to ensure it's aligned to your WHY and your purpose, you need to set your goals, and get them in the right priority order so you can ensure timely implementation of that plan and execution of the actions.

What can a great Accountability Coach provide you with?

Clarity

The foremost benefit of having an Accountability Coach is the ability to generate more clarity. When you work with an Accountability Coach to list and examine your business's strengths and weaknesses, you can pinpoint problem areas and the source of issues. This means that you get more clarity for what you need to do to achieve success and growth.

This in turn gives you a sense of purpose and direction, as you get to know what actions must be taken to fix critical issues in your business and your work environment.

Focus

The benefit of having an Accountability Coach helping you is that you can create a focused and concentrated strategy for dealing with shortcomings and aspects that require immediate attention. You get the ability to focus your energy and thoughts on coming up with solutions that best meet your needs and requirements. An Accountability Coach can also help you get the skillset and training you need to inspire direct action by your staff and employees to address emerging issues and matters that require attention.

Management

The job of an Accountability Coach is not to run your business, but to get you the skills and tools you need to be able to manage your business and work effectively. With the experience you get by strategising planning and prioritising, you can create better management methods and principles that can be successfully applied to any aspect of your work, your business and yourself personally. This benefits your company in the short term and has enormous benefits for future growth and expansion of your business. It's also fantastic for you and your team's professional development and personal growth. Accountability starts at the top, and leaders need to set the right example for others to follow. There's nothing better than management stepping up and setting the example that their staff, teams and others can follow.

Productivity

By streamlining your workflow, teaching yourself and your staff to take responsibility, and creating an environment where accountability is encouraged (hopefully by your leadership), Accountability Coaches can help you increase productivity and bring a positive and optimistic attitude to your workplace.

Be it a multi-national company or a small business, productivity and the proper use of time and resources is vital for success. An Accountability Coach inspires and motivates you and your staff by providing the training to manage stress, workloads, and issues effectively so they can achieve their goals.

Trust

The most important benefit of having an Accountability Coach helping you is the trust you gain in your abilities. With the help of an Accountability Coach, you get a better command of your day-to-day affairs through self-analysis and self-intervention that reflects positively on your company as well as on your staff. In the end, you get a work environment that ensures respect, trust and loyalty through continuous accountability and acceptance.

Such a situation is inherently conducive to progress, as everyone can bring their best to the team and feel that their actions have a positive effect on the company. Now everyone can play their best game.

Finding a great Accountability Partner, Coach or Buddy ensures you will focus attention on working on these clearly identifiable elements; all mission critical to ensure you and your business work in sync and total harmony.

Clearly identifiable elements and outcomes

Create clear goals and objectives

You can sit down with your Accountability Partner, Coach or Buddy and have a long and careful discussion to lay out the specific goals and objectives you are trying to achieve. Sometimes, these goals may not be concrete and may instead be just an idea or a concept. It is your job to have a chat with your Accountability Partner, Coach or Buddy and convert these abstract ideas and concepts into measurable goals that can be readily achieved, with results that can actually be quantified (remember our SMART goals from earlier in the book).

This is important because working on vague ideas cannot provide measurable results, and you will not be sure how far you have come and what you have achieved from your effort. Setting clearly defined goals helps your Accountability Partner, Coach or Buddy keep a check on your progress and creates better goals for more significant achievements.

Provide advice, motivation and insight

Your Accountability Partner, Coach or Buddy is a witness to your progress, effort and journey. With the unique perspective they have on your actions as an independent observer, they can deliver targeted advice and observations to help you smooth out your accountability process. An Accountability Partner, Coach or Buddy is also a source of constant motivation and inspiration.

An Accountability Partner, Coach or Buddy can also help identify problem areas and aspects that require more effort and energy than other factors. In this way, an Accountability Partner, Coach or Buddy serves as a supportive individual familiar with your objectives, and can help you bring meaningful change much more conveniently.

Help you improve your methods

Sometimes, even after trying a lot, we cannot create the desired change or reach an objective easily. At this point, it is common for people to lose energy and motivation and to back down in the face of challenges. Your Accountability Partner, Coach or Buddy can help you take a step back and evaluate a problematic situation from a new perspective. You get the insights you need to determine where energies are being wasted, and what better methods can be utilised to achieve a specific aim. This helps both partners, in the long run, to create a better understanding of each other and themselves, and helps you develop better pathways and methods to deal with challenging situations as they arise along your road to accountability.

Working with an Accountability Partner, Coach or Buddy is an excellent way to bring more motivation, support, and insight to your accountability journey. You and your Accountability Partner, Coach or Buddy can help each other build an understanding of your thoughts and actions, and create ideas to achieve more significant gains in the long run.

I wish all my readers good luck and Godspeed on their accountability journey.

On our road to accountability, just in case the reasons why you need to make an appointment with an Accountability Partner, Coach or Buddy are not clear, let me provide the clarity.

A look from the outside in

An Accountability Partner can be effective if they are from outside your business area. For example, if you're in sales, it might be useful to get an Accountability Partner with experience in human resources.

In this way, you're building yourself as an entrepreneur holistically. They will provide a different perspective on 'sales', or even on how you perceive business. Furthermore, their network will likely be in a different sphere, which you can leverage.

However, I do note that the main purpose of getting an Accountability Partner, Coach or Buddy is not to 'leverage' or use their network, it is to HOLD YOU ACCOUNTABLE to the goals you set for yourself. Do you meet the obligations, promises, goals and commitments made to yourself and others? An Accountability Coach, Business Advisor and Mentor will help.

Remember, it's to get you to START DELIVERING WHAT YOU PROMISE and get your team to do the same.

> **'When a man points a finger at someone else, he should remember that four of his fingers are pointing at himself.'**
> *Louis Nizer*

Not afraid of the tough talks

Another thing you need to look for in an Accountability Partner, Coach or Buddy is someone that is not afraid to tell you 'as it is'. If you're slipping up on your goals or not doing the weekly tasks you were supposed to do, an Accountability Partner, Coach or Buddy should be able to point that out to you directly without any need to be polite or soft.

Remember, before having an Accountability Partner, Coach or Buddy, you were struggling with certain parts of the process of achieving your goals. Your Accountability Partner, Coach or Buddy thus plugs into that process and works on your weaknesses and strengths. They need to be brave to point out any 'excuses, blame and finger pointing' that you may have – they will call you out when you need it.

Creating boundaries

Another important element to consider is how involved you want your Accountability Partner, Coach or Buddy to be. You need to decide what you want to be held accountable for, and how clear you want things to be. Decide which portions of your life you want your Accountability Partner, Coach or Buddy to be involved in.

It would be helpful to mind map ideas to understand what you want to be held accountable for. It could be holistic – for example, fitness, lifestyle, business and career – or it could just be one of them.

You could also use this opportunity to work out arrangements as they relate to the relationship: How long do you want the relationship to last? What's the preferred method of communication? What is the time when you best operate?

The 'so what?'

Finally, agree on what happens when you don't hold up your end of the bargain. What are the consequences of cancelling a meeting? What happens if you don't follow through on your goals?

Remember, your goals are a serious matter. It is something that takes lots of time to achieve. Your Accountability Partner, Coach or Buddy thus needs to be on board and needs to be as serious about you achieving your goals as you are. So, if there are a few occasions where you notice non-commitment from your Accountability Partner, Coach or Buddy, it may be time to cancel and let them go.

Let me introduce you to Andrew Griffiths

I have recorded a Zoom session with my friend and mentor Andrew Griffiths, or AG as I fondly call him. It's a weird kind of moment for me; here I am interviewing my mentor for my fourth book.

Upon reflection, it seems like yesterday, but it was back in 2012 during one of AG's publishing sessions as part of the Dent Global Entrepreneur program that AG inspired me to write in the first place. This is kind of like a 'student interviewing the teacher' moment for me. I hope you enjoy.

Andrew's full bio appears below.

Bonus video

Watch the video recording of my full interview with Andrew conducted over Zoom, due to COVID restrictions and stage-4 isolation at the time of recording, on my website. Please visit: www.tickthoseboxes.com.au/TheAccountabilityAdvantage

Here's my discussion with Andrew.

DARREN: My focus is accountability, and with the name The Accountability Guy® that you so fortunately gave me – many months ago. I remember the night ... I was sitting on your balcony having dinner and a few beers overlooking the City of Melbourne and you called me The Accountability Guy® because my focus is all about accountability.

With this in mind, I wonder how you keep 700-odd first-time authors accountable?

ANDREW GRIFFITHS: Well, I guess there is a couple of things in there. Out of 700, I mean, I've trained a lot more people and not everyone wrote a book. You know, I've been involved in a lot of programs. I mean, I have a good success rate, obviously ... the reality is, what's the difference between someone who does a course and writes a book and someone who does a course and doesn't write a book?

DARREN: What's the difference? How do you identify those people?

ANDREW GRIFFITHS: The people who write a book have a much bigger reason to write the book. They get it, you know. Their 'why' is stronger, they have a bigger motivation. So, someone comes to me and says, 'I want to write a book because I know it's going to be hugely transformational for my business,' they write the book. If you're not convinced of that, you probably won't write the book. I mean, why did you end up writing, after being so adamant that you weren't going to?

DARREN: Because you told me to! But it's correct what you're saying; I think this comes down to the heart of accountability, and that is having a connection to your 'why' and having a connection to your purpose.

ANDREW GRIFFITHS: Absolutely.

DARREN: That was the reason I chose to write my first book, *Honey, let's buy a BOAT!* My why was to explain the process that people did not understand, to show them how easy it was to actually buy a boat. It wasn't difficult if you know these certain key elements. So, my purpose was to educate people and then turn that into a sales opportunity to leverage with my skillset and my business.

ANDREW GRIFFITHS: One of the things I find that is interesting though is that when you're writing a book, for example, it's hard. It's hard to write a book, you know. Definitely it's a hard thing, otherwise everyone would do it. But there's also lots of room for reasons not to write a book. We get busy, who's got the time to write a book, right? You don't write a book during your Monday to Friday 9–5 ... you've got to be prepared to write it on your weekends, at night time, early in the morning.

DARREN: Yeah, put off those plans and prioritise.

ANDREW GRIFFITHS: Exactly. So, it's hard to write a book. You've got to deal with the imposter syndrome. Who the hell am I to write a book? Who's going to read it? What if someone does read it? What if they disagree, what if I look like an idiot?

So, you've got all those reasons – there are plenty of reasons not to write a book. And when we find them, we come up with all the excuses in the world. I'm working with a guy who's been working on his book for 12 years! Never going to write it.

But when your reason for writing is stronger than the reasons not to write it, that's when you write that book. And that's why the power of that 'why', that purpose, 'I need to write this book because it's going to give me a competitive advantage and it's going to transform my business, which means I'm going to be able to feed my family better, I'm going to be able to buy a better car, I'm going to be more successful'. So, the why and the purpose are so important.

DARREN: Andrew, what does the word 'accountability' mean to you?

ANDREW GRIFFITHS: It's interesting, I know we've had many conversations around it. I look at accountability and I guess for me, it's my reason for doing. If I looked at that and said, 'I'm accountable to you, Darren, to finish that,' I will do it because I don't want to let you down. And that's a big enough reason for me.

For people watching and reading this, Darren and I will often catch up for breakfast at 7 o'clock in the morning, and I never give a moment's thought to: 'Will Darren be late?', because Darren is never late. The same thing would happen if I was going to pick Darren up – I would never be late, and he would never worry about me being late because he just knows that it will not happen. Unless it's something out of the ordinary, which I don't think has ever happened. And that's because there's a responsibility to each other. That might seem like a silly or trite example, but it's actually not, because there are people who just can't get in on time, they can't turn up on time, they do can't do what they say.

DARREN: The problem is they don't take on the responsibility to do that task in the first place. So, to use the analogy of me picking you up and we're going for breakfast, we're responsible for things and we're accountable to people. With that premise in mind, I'm responsible for picking you up because I said I was going to do that, and you're going to hold me to account to make sure I do that and I'm not going to let you down. Because that tells you that I don't hold you in enough esteem and enough importance, the fact that you've allocated 7 o'clock in the morning to commit to our get together. So, it's important for us to have that relationship, which is built upon and linked to our purpose.

ANDREW GRIFFITHS: And our respect, and to be honest, our professionalism. It's an interesting kind of thing, but I don't want to disappoint anyone, I don't want to let anyone down. I always remember, one of the keys to success is to say what you'll do and do what you say, as a simple kind of thing because to be honest a lot of people are not very good at that. A lot of people are not very good at delivering on what they've promised.

DARREN: No, they're not. But why is that the case? Why don't you think people do that well enough?

ANDREW GRIFFITHS: Again, I think it comes back to, they need a big enough why. I always say, if I had 100 people in a room and I was going to do a writing program, so you've got 30 days to write your first manuscript, and I'm going to give everyone who does it (finishes their 30,000 words in 30 days) a million dollars, I guarantee I'd have a 100% success rate.

DARREN: It's rather expensive to do that exercise, but why do people make excuses for when they can't do it? So, take the million bucks off the table, and you've got a 30-day writing challenge, you must get a million excuses as to why people didn't do it.

ANDREW GRIFFITHS: And I've used them myself as an author! Like with my publishers, I've had: the crocodile's eaten my manuscript (but I live in Far North Queensland!) in the past. Then I felt that's not appropriate, because I think that being accountable and professional is also something that you develop. You know, I treat my business very seriously, but I believe that as I've gotten older, certainly my reputation and my brand is tied to me delivering. I probably didn't realise that as much when I was younger. At age 54 I know it's very important from me. If I say I'm going to do something, I've got to do something.

DARREN: It's a good example, you're a solo entrepreneur, you love working on your own, it brings the best out of you. And you've got so many products that are coming out, so many new ideas that you're constantly on the front foot delivering stuff for your community. It's relevant, it's stuff that people really want, it solves their problems. How do you stay accountable?

ANDREW GRIFFITHS: It's funny you mention community, because I feel accountable to my community. And that's what this is about. I don't think they make me feel accountable, I don't think that's their task or their intent. But I value my community. These are my customers, people that I've trained, who have bought my books, people I've done business with – I've coached thousands upon thousands of people over the years when you think about it. With my books, hundreds of thousands of people. I feel an obligation, that I choose, to treat my community with respect and value. And part of that is developing the right products; it's how I act, how I go through life, my level of professionalism. All of that stuff, I feel that my community is who I answer to, and I feel accountable to my community. So, I would never do something inappropriate on social media.

If anyone is a customer of mine, I treat them with respect, because they've made a choice. I don't know whether it's old-school, and I mean it, anyone who knows me knows that that is exactly how I am. If you're a member of my community, I'd do anything for you. But in the same vein, I feel that my community would do anything for me. I know they would.

DARREN: Because it's a two-way street – it works so well for the community and for yourself.

ANDREW GRIFFITHS: Exactly, and it's built on mutual respect. I use the argument: would your community fight for you if you needed them to? And I know that my community would. So, it's not like 100 people have gotten together and said, 'We're going to hold you accountable.'

DARREN: No, you've taken that responsibility on yourself because you hold them in such high esteem. Andrew, how do you prioritise what you deliver to your community?

ANDREW GRIFFITHS: I probably don't do it as well as I should, and I have a good Accountability Buddy (you're my Accountability Coach) to help me with that –

DARREN: Thank you, a task I take very seriously and a badge I wear with immense pride!

ANDREW GRIFFITHS: But I guess I do a lot of planning. I do spend a lot of time to keep myself on track. I literally do the yearly plan, quarterly plan, monthly plan, weekly play, daily plan, hourly plan. And people go, 'Oh my God, that's a lot of planning!' But like on a Sunday evening, I'm planning my week. Monday morning I'm planning my day, and at 9 o'clock on Monday morning I'm checking in to make sure I'm on track. 10 o'clock, I just on the hour do a little check in to see whether my day has been derailed yet. I do that to just pull me back on track, because I've got my meaningful, important things that I've got to do today.

Another thing that I do a lot of, I have Mondays where I have no appointments. I have nothing on Monday except my stuff.

DARREN: Yes, how wonderful!

Often when you hear about the term accountability, people think about consequences and penalties. Within your community, how does applying consequences to situations when people who are on a program with you don't do the things they say they're going to do when they're going to do them? How does that sit with you? How do you deal with it?

ANDREW GRIFFITHS: It's challenging for me to answer that, in a couple of ways. One is, I'm so accountability-driven by answering to my community as well. When I'm teaching other people, initially I used to teach people how to dive 35 years ago, and the whole thing is if you teach people how to dive you hope that they're going to go diving. Most people that do a dive course never dive again! That's kind of frustrating, right? So, for me now, if I teach someone to write a book and they don't write a book, initially I think I probably got frustrated ... I probably get a bit grumpy about it.

DARREN: Why would you get grumpy about it?

ANDREW GRIFFITHS: Probably 'frustrated' is the right word, instead of 'grumpy'. It's like, you've got all the tools, you've got all you need, now you can write this book. You came to me; I didn't make you do this course. You've paid your money, you wanted to write a book. But now I've given to you all the information and coaching, but you're not writing. So, there's a bit of frustration in that side of things. But in saying that, for me I do honestly have this concept that I'm teaching adults. I can only do so much, and I actually don't have the patience. I'm not going to treat them like kids.

If they don't do it, then it's their loss. I do everything I can to help them, but then at some stage it's got to be up to them.

DARREN: Because your programs offer so much information and so much follow up, what you're doing (and we talked about this earlier on) is you're removing the excuse element.

ANDREW GRIFFITHS: Yeah.

DARREN: You're removing all that from them – there is no place for them to go other than either do it (if that's what you believe and that's what you want to do), or if you don't want to do it then it's not linked enough to your why (you don't have a big enough reason, you don't get what it's going to do for your business). That's cool, don't do it then.

ANDREW GRIFFITHS: That's it, and you've got to be okay with that. When I first started to teach people how to write books, it's very different to what I do now, because I literally teach what stops people from writing a book. You know, 'I don't find the time' – here's the strategy for finding the time. 'I haven't got enough experience' – okay, here's a framework to show what experience you have. There are ways around all that, and I've developed hundreds of those techniques. You're right, but it does reach a point where it is just simply that their 'why' is not stronger than their reasons 'why not'.

That is the challenge in life for all of us. We all know why I should lose weight – the why has got to be stronger than the why not. Whatever it might be, I think that's the same for all of us. Honestly, I'm too old and too ugly these days to … you know, I'll teach you but what you do with it is up to you.

DARREN: How did you find the writing process for your new book? The man who teaches 700 first-time authors to write their book; how did you find that process for yourself?

ANDREW GRIFFITHS: It's really hard. It made me feel guilty. I mean, I had a book coming out a couple of years ago, but it was a bit different. It was a collection of articles, probably been about eight years since my last book-book. But this one was hard to write, because I'm really busy, all the reasons, but also the weight of the book. And again, the accountability. You know, when you've got 700 people who you've taught to write books, you're telling me they're not looking at your book with that extra...

DARREN: The bar has gone up to such a height.

ANDREW GRIFFITHS: And I feel that responsibility and accountability to all these people who I've taught to write books and tutored and got them to write. I look at that and go: there's no cutting corners on this book, no excuses from me. Again, though, I'm accountable to my community of authors.

ANDREW GRIFFITHS: Yeah. The why, I mention in my book: the bigger the why the smaller the obstacles. That's the way that it seems to go – when our obstacles are bigger than our why, it is never going to work. It's out of balance. If they're about the same, it could go either way. But I know chatting with someone within a few minutes whether or not they're going to write a book. I know with their language and their body language and how they talk about where they're at, simply because when they get that moment, they find a big enough why. They've just got to hang onto that why.

DARREN: Taking all you just said into account, when I stood up in that classroom and put up my hand and said I wasn't going to be writing a book, did you ever think I'd write four of them?

ANDREW GRIFFITHS: I never thought you'd write four of them, but I thought you'd write one. I really did. I loved the fact that you got up and said that in the class, because I wasn't going to let you not write one. That was like a challenge, that was like the red flag to the bull.

DARREN: It ties back to accountability again, because what I did also was I got up there in front of the class, put myself out on a pedestal, you put me back in my box and gave me the whack around the head that I deserved, and I thought, 'I'm going to write a book and prove him wrong! I'll show him I can do it.' So, you flipped it all the way around. There's a great lesson of accountability; tell people what you're going to do, make a big scene in front of an audience, and then make sure you save face by delivering.

ANDREW GRIFFITHS: Was that any different with your third book? When you and I were talking in a restaurant about writing your third book, I said, 'Okay, if you finish it by this date, we'll do a launch for you in Bali.' And this was like 3 1/2 months before – it was a really tight schedule, and you're going to launch it on a beach in Bali. I've got an author retreat, there's a whole pile of people that are going to be there, it's going to be on the beach, it's going to be awesome – but no book, no launch!

DARREN: No book, no launch, and guess what! There's the photo, right above my head in my office, of you and I sitting on that wonderful beach. That was just before the fireworks went off!

ANDREW GRIFFITHS: So, we had fireworks on the beach in Bali.

DARREN: Full moon, it was magnificent!

ANDREW GRIFFITHS: Again, the reason that you wrote your book was not so much about doing the launch in Bali, but you felt accountable to me.

DARREN: I did, absolutely. I put myself out there and made a commitment, and as soon as I made that commitment – it's advice for everybody listening, tell as many people as you can that you're going to go and do something (carry out a task, an action, a goal), because they will work with you. You wanted me to succeed. You didn't want me to be proven wrong, you wanted me to be there in Bali to have that book launch, so I was going to do everything I possibly could to make that happen because I had made a commitment to you and also you wanted me to succeed so you helped me through it. We worked together at a common goal. That's just such a wonderful outcome.

ANDREW GRIFFITHS: Don't you think sometimes people do get this accountability thing a little bit muddled up? They don't realise that no one wants to see you fail, they want to see you succeed.

DARREN: 100%, I'm on their team and my their success is my success. We are in this together.

ANDREW GRIFFITHS: What I like about how we worked together from an accountability point of view, is it's about helping each other to succeed, not going: 'Why didn't you do it?' That's not the conversation. It's like: 'How can I help you do that?'

DARREN: And we turned it around. It doesn't have that negative connotation that we're doing accountability because you need extra help. It's saying, 'Hang on, how can we together with our experience and our understanding pull it together and work as a team for a common goal?' That's ultimately what a team is all about, it's picking your team members who have different skillsets (the way you and I are different), and we all come together as one to focus on a common goal.

ANDREW GRIFFITHS: Absolutely. Another part of this is respect. I think respect is huge. The way that you're using accountability, is if you've got people that you respect. I respect my community, I respect you, I respect my publishers, I respect my clients, I respect people. And that respect I treat very seriously ... it's important for me. I don't need them to hold me accountable, I don't need you to hold me accountable, you just do because I respect you and we work together. So, it's not like I'm answering to you, it's we're collaborating to achieve this.

DARREN: Correct. I think that's why having an Accountability Partner, Buddy, friend, that is not a social friend of yours, is not your spouse, is not your life partner, but to find someone that jells with us on those levels, that can go and have that hard conversation with you. To call you out when you need it, we all need it. Your partner has permission to do that with you. That's why having someone at arm's-length works so much better than having a friend or a colleague.

ANDREW GRIFFITHS: Because what we end up in that case, I think we often end up with misery buddies. No problem with having a misery buddy, but you still need an Accountability Buddy. Your misery buddy is going to say, 'Oh, I know you've had a rough week, I get that.' That's awesome, it makes you feel good, but it doesn't get stuff done.

The Andrew Griffiths Story

Who exactly is Andrew Griffiths? Isn't he the hugely successful kids' author who writes hilarious titles like *The Day My Bum Went Psycho* – a huge hit? Naturally, with a title like that, Andy gets young kids interested in reading in the first instance. All this with much support from the education departments and teachers from all over this country. And with good reason … Nope, wrong Andrew Griffiths.

There's the kids' author called Andy Griffiths, and I'm with the other one, who is more relevant to our businesses: Andrew Griffiths, the business author. Andrew who teaches us older kids (the adults) to run better businesses and be better people in the process.

Today, Andrew is known for being an international bestselling author and a global presenter. Of course, Andrew was an overnight success, right? Well, like most overnight successes, where Andrew is today is the end result of a lot of hard work, taking more than his fair share of risks, falling over often but always getting back up, dusting himself off, learning his lessons and keeping on going. Over many years, Andrew has learned and perfected three really important keys to success: resilience, belief and determination. Master these and everything changes.

It has been 20 years since Andrew's first book, the iconic *101 Ways to Market Your Business* (Allen & Unwin), first hit the shelves. The success of this book led to a suite of other business titles, media interviews (over 500), podcast interviews and much more. Andrew's books have been translated into languages as diverse as Nigerian, Chinese, Indonesian, Russian and Indian.

Andrew's advice is a combination of street-smart wisdom, practical concepts and productive triggers, derived from the hard-learned lessons with his own trial and error, as well as years of close observation and identification of the characteristics shared by both the really successful and the really unsuccessful.

Andrew started his business world at the age of 18 as a commercial diver. He taught bush survival skills in the outback of Western Australia, ran his own travel business, his own SCUBA school, an advertising business, and most recently a marketing consultancy.

Described by many as the big man with the big heart, Andrew is on a mission to share the entrepreneurial rites of passage that he has experienced to help others set themselves apart from the crowd and to stay relevant with their customers for a lifetime. In a world where simply keeping up is proving a great challenge, hearing about what is happening with both the big business world and the small business world from someone with 35 years of entrepreneurial experience is hugely beneficial. Thoroughly engaging, a masterful speaker with decades of experience on stages around the world, and one of the leading entrepreneurial speakers in Australia, Andrew is the man that over 500 organisations have trusted to help inspire, challenge and engage their audiences.

Andrew is able to share his observations, experiences and research from around the world to identify the exact steps any organisation needs to take to become future proof. And he delivers his advice in a down-to-earth, simple and often hilarious way. Andrew's been an entrepreneurial commentator for many years, sharing both his observations and his realisations with audiences including inc.com out of New York, American-based media giant CBS, NewsCorp and many others.

> **'Accountability and self-responsibility are critical to our success in personal, professional and public life. However, we often look for those character traits in others, rather than inculcating them in ourselves.'**
> *Vishwas Chavan*

Chapter 7

Review process

100% is right in your sights –
it's so close, you can almost taste it.

100%

The Road to Accountability

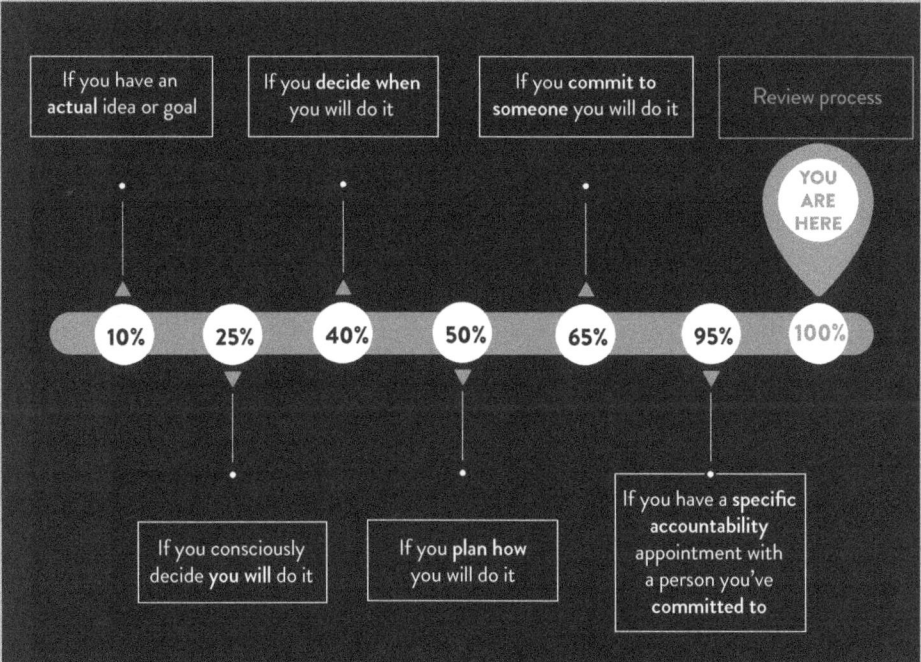

If you have an **actual** idea or goal

If you **decide when** you will do it

If you **commit to someone** you will do it

Review process

YOU ARE HERE

10% 25% 40% 50% 65% 95% 100%

If you consciously decide **you will** do it

If you **plan how** you will do it

If you have a **specific accountability** appointment with a person you've **committed to**

Based on the 2010 study conducted by the American Society of Training and Development (ASTD).

Surely by now, you have noticed that I'm really into using these two central words: implementation and execution. Why I'm such a fan of both and why it's so important on our road to accountability is that over the course of the past few years, I've been asking clients during our sessions what these words mean to them. Here's the results, which are applicable to this part of our journey on our road to accountability.

Implementation and execution are two distinct phases in the process of carrying out a plan or project. While they are related and often interconnected, they have different focuses and objectives. Here are the key differences between implementation and execution:

☑ **Implementation:** It's about putting a plan into action, setting up resources, and establishing the necessary groundwork.

☑ **Execution:** It's the actual performance of tasks to achieve the desired results within a specified time-frame. It focuses on following procedures and making real-time decisions.

My former boss Steve Jobs once said, "To me, ideas are worth nothing unless executed"... Execution is worth millions. "Even, if you brainstorm a brilliant strategy, it will all be wasted if it's never fully brought to fruition." Wise words, Steve.

Review sessions with your Accountability Partner, Coach or Buddy are critical for you to stay focused, stay on track, and ensure timely implementation and execution.

The best way to ensure that you implement and execute your plan properly is to break down the elements to match what we have discussed previously, in chapters 1 to 6 on our road to accountability.

To refresh your memory and put this to the forefront of your thinking, let us consider what we have covered so far with the most important messages and takeaways.

Chapter 1 – Identify what needs to be done

Moves you to 10% – if you have an actual
idea or goal, this is where you'll begin.

Before you become too concerned whether you are **G**etting **S**h!t **D**one or being productive, ask yourself the following questions:

- ☑ Do you have clear-cut goals?

- ☑ What is it that you want to achieve and when?

- ☑ What is your WHY, and ensure that's linked back to your purpose?

- ☑ Then, ensure your daily efforts are aligned with your goals.

This chapter will help you identify clear goals that you can execute effectively.

We covered four key components:

- ☑ Decide what is NOT important, and declutter your mind.

- ☑ Learn to say NO!

- ☑ Determine your values and visualise.

- ☑ Design your SMART goals.

Chapter 2 – Decide it's important that you do

Moves you to 25% – if you consciously decide you will do it.

In chapter 2, we learned how to trust your gut, your head, your heart, and finally trust your decision. You'll become super clear on your goal; everything else will fall in place behind it.

We covered four key components:

- ☑ How to trust your gut.

- ☑ How to trust your head.

- ☑ How to trust your heart.

- ☑ How to trust your decisions.

Chapter 3 – Set priorities

***Moves you to 40% – if you decide
when you will do it.***

You're now at the point where you have set goals, and consciously thought them through. A potential stumbling block to achieving this may be your ability to prioritise your goals. In chapter 3 we learned how to prioritise your goals.

We covered three key components:

- ☑ Put your list in ONE place.
- ☑ Darren's 5D's (Do, Delay, Delegate, Delete, or ask Darren).
- ☑ Eating the biggest frog first.

Chapter 4 – Plan what needs to be done and how you will do it

Moves you to 50% – if you plan how you will do it.

Understand the importance of planning, putting a thought process down before you start anything, and using your time to your advantage.

Remember, the idea is always to reduce the total amount of time you are working in half, or even more.

We covered three key components:

- ☑ Scheduling your tasks.
- ☑ Evaluating your progress.
- ☑ Common pitfalls and why you may fail.

Chapter 5 – Tell the world

*Moves you to 65% – if you commit
to someone you will do it.*

Understand the importance of committing to someone else, other than yourself, to hold you accountable for the goals you set. Remember, the idea is to achieve all the goals you set for yourself.

We covered three key components:

☑ Who should you share your goals with?

☑ The ins and outs of Accountability Partners.

☑ When to share your goals

Chapter 6 – Find a person to hold you to account

*Moving you to 95% – if you have a
specific accountability appointment
with a person you've committed to.*

An Accountability Partner, Coach or Buddy provides you with specific feedback to support you and track your goals alongside you.

It's a real bonus if you can find an Accountability Coach who can also be your mentor. I show you how and what you should pay attention to.

We covered four key components:

☑ The true meaning of accountability.

☑ How to make accountability a habit.

☑ How to find an Accountability Partner.

☑ Group Accountability Forums.

Once we have set ourselves targets, it is crucial that we review them regularly to ensure that we are on track. But how regularly would best suit top performances? Is it; daily, weekly, monthly, quarterly or annually?

The ultimate purpose of any review, not just a target review – and don't get me wrong; the numbers are really important – is to ensure that we do not forget something important to us: a promise you made and an obligation to be fulfilled, an important customer proposal, the creation of a webinar, the date of publication of your new book, whatever it is.

Verifying goals with your Accountability Coach is no exception – it helps us remember our *important goals*, not some new, bright, shiny object that seems like a good idea at the time, but something that we are determined to address.

Symptoms of a non-serious goal can be:

☑   You have no plans on how to achieve it (you're too lazy to work on it).

☑   It's not your priority at the moment (you're too busy to work on it).

Goals like this should be discarded, instead of reviewed, so that you can direct your attention to goals that truly matter, like we've reviewed and identified with our SMART goals in the first chapter.

Before you talk to your coach, check all your goals, and make sure you only review the goals you are serious about achieving. Something you know you *need to do*, not something you think you *can't do* until you have at least considered your priorities and whether they actually fit your list of priorities.

> ### 'Make yourself accountable and your employees will hold themselves to a high standard.'
> *David J. Greer*

Frequency of engagement and sessions

Now it's time for execution – I bet that statement got your attention.

To do this in the most effective manner, you have to set the frequency of how often you will meet with your Accountability Partner, Coach or Buddy. There's discussion from all parts of business (Google it and you'll see) and much debate and deliberation about *how often* you should get together with your coach. Opinions vary, some say weekly, others fortnightly, monthly, there's quarterly, half yearly and even as far out as annually. I guess it depends on your purpose.

The most accurate answer to this question can be found by talking to my clients and asking them about where they have received the most tangible value from my private One-On-One program. I have spoken to a broad range of clients, all seeking a common undertaking to achieve their goals and tasks.

Almost all my clients, some 91.6%, have engaged me for a fixed period of 12 months, and components such as our Weekly Check-Ins and our monthly and longer One-On-One sessions work very well indeed. Underpinned with the road to accountability framework, this is the basis of their decision to proceed with me and my program.

Frequency and longevity of working with your Accountability Partner or Buddy or the engagement of your Accountability Coach are paramount as you build a relationship and collectively work on the achievement of a set of goals which have been agreed. Long-term coaching commitments are common in business coaching and other forms of personal coaching, including health, recovery, personality development and life coaching.

Minimum lengths of client engagements are typically six months – less than that and the customer is unlikely to experience desired outcomes and not realise the value of continuing. In addition, the coach is likely to be stuck on a carousel, constantly striving to build momentum and stay up to date with the client's activities, practices and nuances.

For me, my 6-month and 12-month programs, which are my most popular, offer my clients a significant opportunity to engage in the wonderfully regular routine, which is an excellent opportunity to break old habits and achieve tangible and measurable results moving forward.

Because my 12-month program is a whole year with me, we can get things done and can achieve your goals and complete your projects and tasks decisively.

That's 60 sessions, with one Weekly Check-In each week (48) plus our longer One-On-One session on a monthly basis (12) totals 60, over a 12-month period. By working directly with me on your business, I'll keep you accountable and ensure you deliver on your promises, goals and commitments you've made to others, and to yourself. We'll meet your deadlines, achieve your goals and outcomes. With my success in this area, I cannot afford to risk my reputation by making promises that I cannot keep, or doing anything other than achieving incredible results.

It is this philosophy and trust in the road to accountability that has enabled me to achieve 97.8 customer satisfaction, countless glossy reviews and significant results for companies around the world.

Perhaps most importantly, my system is based on proven principles, frameworks, and strategies that have helped countless business owners and executives become truly accountable and grow in all sorts of new ways.

To address how you should meet with your Accountability Partner, Coach or Buddy, let's take a look at how my current program works as an example. For all my clients, whether interstate or international, all my sessions are carried out using Zoom. This suits everyone particularly well. We can share screens to review spreadsheets, sales forecasts and to review their marketing programs and the supporting data. We will use the whiteboard feature and breakout rooms in Zoom when I am working with teams. This works particularly well, and I'm a big fan, and no, I'm not on commission from Zoom, I know it sounds like I am. The simplicity of recording a Zoom session, naturally with client approval, is both beneficial for the client and coach, and is to be encouraged. It is really healthy to go back and review earlier session recordings; to refresh your understanding of an agreed strategy, to provide clarity or to get a solid understanding of what was agreed, especially the selected due dates.

Also, you know I'm from Melbourne and at the time of writing this book we are in serious stage-4 COVID lockdown, yet other major cities here in Australia are not. So, it's business as usual for me with my clients – we can use Zoom regardless of their location, or circumstances.

However, I'm still a big fan of visiting my clients face to face at some stage early in the engagement to establish a concrete connection. I feel you learn a lot by visiting their workplace and observing their environment. It's also delightful to build relationships with their teams, to place a face to the name as we meet in person. I would encourage a face-to-face session at some point in your relationship with your Accountability Partner, Coach or Buddy, if that is at all possible.

What does an Accountability Session entail?

Let's understand the process in more detail:

Private One-On-One Session:

- ☑ Ideally, and what's most popular, are my One-On-One sessions for one hour each and every week via Zoom.

- ☑ We talk strategy, sales, competitor analysis, marketing, communications, finances and staff (your team performance) and anything else my clients wish to talk about. You'll set the agenda, or I can work with you and we'll set it together.

- ☑ During these sessions we will set and agree on your goals and plans, and review your priorities and set the timelines for the month(s) ahead.

- ☑ We can discuss your team, staff and personal relationships, whatever you feel needs to be addressed.

- ☑ We will review the last quarter, last business year to answer the five critical questions we talked about earlier.

- ☑ They are:
    - ✓ Where exactly are you now?

The Accountability Advantage

- ✓ Where do you want to be?
- ✓ What's been stopping you?
- ✓ How do you want to get there?
- ✓ Why is this an absolute must for you?

Weekly Check-Ins:

- ☑ I'll personally call you every week to check in on your progress and review your implementation and execution.

- ☑ This is a check-in call to your preferred number (usually mobile or Zoom) at a set time each and every week. This keeps you on your toes and holds you to account so you 'do the things you say you are going to do', and are 'getting your team to do the same.'

- ☑ My calls ensure you complete your agreed actions, tasks and promises on time, and I'll personally hold you to account.

- ☑ I'll provide you with support, advice, counsel and encouragement.

- ☑ I find that clients love the notion of getting a task completed prior to the due date as they don't want to let me down or take their hands off the wheel. Works fine for everyone; that's a real win/win.

Session Notes and Action Items (optional, as most clients prefer to take their own notes):

- ☑ Everything we discuss gets documented. For review purposes, our Zoom sessions will be recorded and available to you, if you wish via Dropbox.

- ☑ Within two business days of our sessions, you will receive your personalised 'Session Notes & Action Items'.

- ☑ This is so you can review the session and ensure your follow-up items and your to-do's are agreed and recorded, so you can tick those boxes once you have successfully executed each of them.

☑ Nothing gets overlooked or missed.

☑ You can run, but you cannot hide.

Following every One-On-One and Weekly Check-In, the client shall be emailed a copy of our Session Notes and Action Items within two business days following the session.

Just like the formal Board of Management papers, minutes always follow a meeting, it formalises what is discussed and agreed with those in attendance. It sets the standard and the level of professionalism and importance of what we are doing for which we both operate.

To ensure the Session Notes and Action Items correctly reflect the session discussion, and to confirm the client's willingness and acceptance to complete the Action Items listed, and confirm they will do so by return email. This is an important step in gaining a commitment to a specific task and due date, ensuring the client takes on, and accepts the task and actions required.

This removes potential excuses which means we have NO misunderstandings. Failure isn't an option for either of us.

Cloud-based measurement:

☑ Each client will receive 24/7 access to our shared, cloud-based DropBox for the recording of your Action Items with what needs to be done, and what has been done.

☑ Activity and progress measurement so we can all keep track and you can invite your team members to administer to join in, if required.

☑ Some clients prefer to take their own Session Notes and Action Items. No problem, the choice is yours.

Resources access:

☑ We have plenty of free, super helpful downloads to help you stay on track.

Direct access:

☑ Depending on the coaching package you've selected, you may have direct access to me outside of our sessions times by: phone, text, WhatsApp or by email. Check out my coaching programs to see the options which are available.

☑ Ideal for support, encouragement, counsel, clarity, review and questions.

Calendar entries and date selection

Session dates, times, location or the chosen virtual platform e.g. Zoom and must be agreed with your Accountability Partner, Coach or Buddy in advance, and diary invitations will be sent.

Clients have requested that I set up a 'repeating calendar event' by using Google Calendar; my personal preference, as it works seamlessly across the majority of online calendars and schedules, and goes straight into your diary which you or your team can manage.

This helps manage our times better and avoids other conflicting engagements in your diary. Again, we remove potential roadblocks and excuses for non-completion of assigned tasks.

It's also easy to add, say, the Zoom link and password and/or specific external address for sessions for the entire period of engagement.

It's also paramount that this event is a priority in one's life, and common sense should prevail. This means your accountability session MUST take precedence and priority over all other matters except for:

☑ personal injury or family emergency

☑ annual leave or a business trip (naturally, having advised the dates in advance)

☑ being too ill (or contagious) to attend.

The role of the client is to:

- ☑ Be punctual for each session, ensuring you arrive on time and with 100% focus. Constantly being late is both unprofessional and unacceptable.

- ☑ Complete action items and agreed commitments made during and between our coaching sessions.

- ☑ Be open to new ideas.

- ☑ Be ready to take action and make quick decisions.

- ☑ Make the program a priority.

- ☑ Be prepared, and make time for the work that you need to do for the sessions/programs or services.

- ☑ Trust the process.

- ☑ Take responsibility for your outcomes.

- ☑ Ask any questions as they arise.

- ☑ Give permission for your Accountability Coach to have those tough conversations with you, to call you out when needed, and to question you if you are not doing the things to have agreed to by the due dates that you agreed and set.

The role of the Accountability Coach is to:

- ☑ Come to each session/program prepared.

- ☑ Devote my full attention to you during the coaching sessions/programs or services.

- ☑ Stretch you outside of your comfort zone into new areas and support you as you do so.

- ☑ Provide you with resources and knowledge for your business endeavours.

- ☑ Provide a safe space where you can express yourself and be heard.

- ☑ Challenge you to create the business you want.

☑ Offer support, encouragement, feedback, and guidance throughout the sessions/programs or services.

☑ Help you turn your goals into practical measurable actions.

Goals are fundamentally ideas that you want to come true. Remember: '**A GOAL WITHOUT A PLAN IS ONLY A WISH**'.

To make them happen, you need to break down every goal into practical actions so you get closer to your milestone. If your goal is to find a reliable local manufacturer, it's not going to happen until you do your research, make some calls, set up interviews, and evaluate each from multiple perspectives.

An Accountability Coach comes in with significant business experience and has the ability to solve this problem for you. They will define a clear path that you can follow to achieve a certain business goal and work together with your until you achieve it.

> **'Open collaboration encourages greater accountability, which in turn fosters trust.'**
> *Ron Garan*

Keeps you away from distractions and procrastination

Your Accountability Coach isn't merely a planner; they also keep you honest and true to your word. Once they have outlined a plan for you, the Accountability Coach checks in on a regular basis to ensure that you have done what you said you were going to do. When you have this feeling of someone asking questions looming over your head, you are less likely to procrastinate or get distracted. This doesn't only save you time, but you find yourself making quick progress towards your desired goals.

Evaluates your progress and provides feedback

Oftentimes, entrepreneurs aren't sure if what they are doing is actually adding value. With an Accountability Coach you don't have to deal with that type of uncertainty and doubt. As an experienced business professional, the Accountability Coach doesn't only evaluate your actions and progress but also provides instant feedback to ensure you stay on the right track. They may ask you to shuffle your priorities or provide advice where they think you can do better.

Your Accountability Coach will also go through the Action Items and follow-ups from your previous session and review your progress and completion to ensure you are meeting those deadlines, your goals and commitments you've promised to other people and those meaningful items and tasks you've promised yourself.

Celebrates your wins and lends a shoulder when going gets tough

Business is all about winning some, and losing some.

Whatever the case may be, your Accountability Coach stays by your side to celebrate your achievements and milestones. However, when things don't go your way, they are there to provide you the moral support you need to get back up and bounce back with all you've got. We've got your back.

Create a feedback loop

To complete the entire process, you must create a feedback loop for yourself that answers the following questions:

- ☑ Am I more accountable than when I started this process?
- ☑ Is this still working for me?
- ☑ Are there any notable improvements?

To answer these questions, you need to be continually reviewing your process. From the external and internal environment, you then need to use it to improve your process – whether it be your goal-setting process or your Accountability Partner sessions.

Some goals are long term, and others short term, and as such can be achieved by the end of the day. So, you must have a solid review process to know it's working.

A goal tracker

As mentioned earlier, you need a tracker to track what you are doing. If it isn't measurable, then it's probably not a goal. At all times, your Accountability Coach should look at your tracker and understand where you are. You can use terms like 'right on track' or 'late' to pursue your goals.

Use this simple TICK BOX exercise to review your process and goals:

- ☑ The goal is taking too much time.
- ☑ The goal is no longer relevant.
- ☑ My Accountability Coach is helping me.
- ☑ My Accountability Coach has helped me improve my process.
- ☑ I have different habits to the ones before I started.
- ☑ I have failed a few times along the way.

There are no right or wrong answers to the above. It is used positively to make you think about what feedback you need to take to improve what you are doing.

I don't think there's anything more competitive in today's world than being an entrepreneur. It requires you to devote all you have – from your time, your comfort zone, your money and your resources, begged, borrowed and stolen (I hope not). All lined up for you to make your summit attempt. To have a shot at being successful so you can achieve financial freedom and greater choices in life. Engaging an Accountability Partner, Coach or Buddy gives you the competitive advantage by keeping you motivated and on your toes at all times, so you can push for the summit and hit your 100%.

When you finally reach the summit, **STOP**, breathe and admire the view as you take it in. They say the journey is the reward, and you've hit the summit, so it's time to take stock, set your next goal to achieve, and please set it with a decent stretch from what you've achieved today now that you understand the steps and framework required to achieve your goals.

Congratulations, now simply repeat your journey on the road to accountability and continue to smash your goals like glass piñatas ...

Let me introduce you to Chris Robb

I have recorded a Zoom session with Chris who is a fantastic guy who takes on monumental projects with such enthusiasm and passion. Chris has a wonderful level of optimism, and he always delivers his completed projects in spades and with a level of ease. Chris is an author, dynamic International Speaker, High Impact Consultant and CEO of Mass Participation World.

Chris gets up each morning to spread the incredible life-changing lessons of his 30 years in the mass participation sports industry so that he can help and inspire others to create a powerful impact on our world in their own personal and business lives. He has already impacted the lives of millions of people through delivering events across three continents.

Chris's full bio appears below.

Bonus video

Watch the video recording of my full interview with Chris conducted over Zoom, due to COVID restrictions and stage-4 isolation at the time of recording, on my website. Please visit: www.tickthoseboxes.com.au/TheAccountabilityAdvantage

Here's my discussion with Chris.

DARREN: Chris, my focus is on accountability. I'm really fascinated by the role of accountability and how that plays with your teams and your stakeholders when you're putting together a major event like your Singapore Marathon, 60,000 participants, 5,000 volunteers – how do you bring that sort of thing together?

CHRIS ROBB: It's a great question and obviously something I'm very passionate about and very lucky to have had the opportunity to be at the helm of an event like that. I think at the real outset it's being very clear on what your objectives are; and there are obviously many of them in an event like that.

If you just start with who your stakeholders are, from your internal stakeholders of your staff, your team. I mean, I'm out of the business that used to organise that, I sold it to IRONMAN about four years ago now. But I would have a full-time team of 30 staff, and as we grew toward the event that would build to

5,000 staff and volunteers on event day, which is pretty huge and you've then got to communicate differently with all of them.

But then there's all these external stakeholders that you are impacting.

You're shutting down a busy city like Singapore, as in the case with these major events. You're impacting hotels, you're impacting places of worship, you're impacting hospitals, normal little businesses, the people who usually on a Sunday morning would get up and walk across the road and buy their newspaper or have their bowl of noodles, and people that are travelling to catch up with family and friends. So, there is a lot of thinking and planning and on-the-ground work that has to be done to engage with all of those stakeholders.

One of the key elements is engagement; coming back to the whole theme of accountability, you can't expect to have people accountable, I believe, unless you've engaged them first. Whether that's engaging with your core team, your volunteers, your clients in terms of sponsors and so on, your participants (they obviously play a huge part in that). Talk about it from a customer perspective. Imagine you run a business that went from fundamentally zero customers to 60,000 in the space of four to five months, sometimes as little as three to four months, and if you haven't engaged them and held them accountable to some degree, it's not just the 5,000 staff, it's the 60,000 people and the millions of people in the city around them that you're hoping will be accountable in some way to support the event.

DARREN: You mentioned engagement is the place it begins. Can we talk a little bit more about how you go about getting engagement, firstly at a staff level before you then expand that to a bigger audience? Where does engagement start for you?

CHRIS ROBB: I think, most importantly, it's being able to engage with the team to ensure you're all on the same vision and have the same objective – which in our case was to deliver a safe and enjoyable event. So, we're all onboard to be to be able to deliver that. Then in terms of what our responsibility is with each of our functional areas and how we interplay with each other. The saying that I use so often in our industry: you're only as good as your weakest link. You get something wrong in a group like that and you're up the creek without a paddle, so to speak.

So, it's making sure everyone is brought into the objective, then in terms of detail it's building a very detailed timeline and plan.

Obviously when you get to an event like the Singapore marathon, which is a repeat event, it is a lot easier because you've got timelines and game charts and all those things in place, and you're just tweaking them year by year. But when you've got that blank piece of canvas and you're starting at the very beginning, it's a matter of being very clear on the different elements that everyone has to do and how you capture those and put in a timeline, and in a way that everyone buys into it.

I had the great privilege and opportunity to work on the Sydney Olympics. I was the event supervisor at the Sydney Olympics.

An incredible life memorable experience. We had all these similar things, but the software that had been prescribed by the so-called Sydney organising committee was something that everyone hated. Every month we got to a stage where it was: okay, it's accountability date and everyone would go retrospectively fitting their tasks in there to make sure they made these key timelines. Really superfluous at the end of the day, but people would be forced to do something.

And in the bigger scheme of things, obviously it needed to be done because you've got all the other sports and everything else; but without that buy in it became a process where we literally had our own software, we were running our own timelines. And that created issues for everyone.

If you haven't got the clarity of vision, the communication of the vision from an engagement perspective, and then the tools to be able to help people to achieve that, you're going to inevitably run into some roadblocks.

DARREN: You talked about the weakest link; your team is only as good as the weakest link. How do you identify what the weakest link is? Because that's not always visible.

CHRIS ROBB: There's two ways to do so. Identify it with the mindset that goes in expecting, not in a negative sense, but being prepared to expect that something will go wrong.

DARREN: Expect the unexpected.

CHRIS ROBB: Expect the unexpected. We do huge amounts of scenario planning; table toping to try and identify and role-play different things that might be able to happen. So, you can identify those on a personal level, to say: well, we're not confident that that particular manager is on top of their game, and then to be able to sit down and work together and provide support and engagement. And then to go into this with the mindset not that we're expecting failure, but that we're prepared that something is going to go wrong.

Absolutely inevitable in an event of that complexity, the large numbers shared, the multiple stakeholders that you're dealing with, closing the city, outdoors you're open to the nuances of weather. You have no control over that.

Then the other part of the narrative working in Asia – and I've had the incredible privilege of being based in Asia for 16–17 years now – is that you have these very different cultural nuances that you need to deal with as well. For example, in many Asian cultures, 'face' as we call it is really important. So, making sure that you don't put people in a position where they lose face, and when there is a problem you've got to deal with it in such a way that you're not embarrassing someone because you then lose them off the bus, so to speak.

Again, it comes back to that whole engagement piece, in that how do you engage when something hasn't been done right? How do you engage with a weakest link potential type of person without making them feel they're going to lose face?

You know, I've got it wrong many times and sometimes even still do, albeit that I'm not still running that business. Interpreting those nuances in different countries is really important.

DARREN: Fasinating, it truly is … How do you find the idea of staff buddying with each other to keep each other accountable in the process? Does that work, is something you've investigated?

CHRIS ROBB: Yes. Sometimes buddying people directly, particularly giving a more junior person the opportunity to be buddied with someone else; but more I think creating a smaller kind of team environment in that situation. We have situations where we do a lot of training. So most of those 5,000 volunteers need to attend one training day, and that kind of goes from a broader big group where there's a lecture type thing in the broader principle, and then breaking that into smaller groups and being in a position where we would do these roleplays or table tops where we literally say the course guys are sitting in that room with a radio and the venue guys are here and the marketing guys here, the risk management guys here.

Then you literally sit for hours on the radio, saying: the guest of honour is running half an hour late, what are we going to do, or whatever. So that buddying happens more in a group situation.

Often, for example, you take an aide station, which is where you give out drinks, you might have 20 to 30 staff that are working on that, and they've got a leader who fits into a hierarchy.

They would buddy up more probably, and in a little core group that's working on that particular area. In the core team of the full-time staff, absolutely they were mentors that looked after each of their more junior people. I would mentor my senior management people and have that buddying process, but when you get to that level it's more of a group accountability that you work towards.

DARREN: How does a group get together and set the priorities for what needs to be done? From an outsider's perspective, there must be so many things that you need to get into an order of priority.

CHRIS ROBB: It's lots of hours in boardrooms, it's white boarding. As I said, as you get down the track and you're repeating the event, you've got a template that you've used.

So, you're in a position where you're not reinventing a huge amount of it. Albeit I had a situation at one stage where my operations director left me, took my entire operations team and set up a competing business.

We literally had five months to build a new operations team, fundamentally. There was one or two people that stayed behind, we had our whole marketing team intact and the operations team had moved off to set up a competing business. So, we were kind of reinventing the wheel again. So, there was an element of saying: we have to take the process of this is how we do it, this is how we're going to do it, and there was that level of urgency. It was a stressful period of time; a new operations director was coming up to speed with senior managers in that team.

Coming back to your question, how do you agree on what those priorities are; in that situation you have to be much more top line, and say: this is the stuff we've done for years; we're going to stick with it and move through it, this is kind of the plan. Documenting, training, but at the very beginning it's being very clear on these are the top line things we want to achieve, then of course timelining that and charting to make sure that you understand where the overlaps are. And there's obviously a system of, you start with the marketing and there's a whole bunch of stuff that comes before the marketing, but there's a bunch of operations things you need in that marketing. So, you kind of announce the event and give the marketing people the tools they want, if you haven't got some degree of finality. Like you said, lots and lots of moving parts that are fitting into the jigsaw.

DARREN: Consequences for when things don't go well, consequences for not being held to account, do they apply to this? Do they apply in your business?

CHRIS ROBB: Absolutely, massive consequences. You've got an event with the numbers of we've spoken about, that's being broadcast globally. You are in a position at 4:30 am when the marathon starts, you need to be ready to go live on TV. So, the consequences of getting that wrong, where you don't start on time, has this massive knock-on effect. Or little things along the way, and in these days of social media that gets picked up and amplified very quickly. You know, an aide station running out of water or runners being sent the wrong way, or long queues at the baggage or long queues at the check-in – before you know it that's being Tweeted and Facebooked and is on Instagram, and the consequences can be enormous.

Then you have the very real consequence of people doing something that's incredibly arduous. I've dealt with five people dying on my watch over the years, and that's obviously a massive consequence, not only in terms of the responsibility, the impact that it has on your team from a mental and emotional perspective.

And then the media element of that, every one of them is played out differently when one of them never made it into the media and another one was a front-page media story, and then that puts into a whole bunch of responsibility and accountability that you're dealing with.

DARREN: How did you address the responsibility point of view? If you look yourself in the mirror and think you played a role in it?

CHRIS ROBB: Yeah. I think inevitably the buck stops with me at the top of the organisation. I've always been one of those people who is prepared to put my hand up and acknowledge. I mean, sometimes it's taken me a month or two to say I didn't do that right, but I believe I'm a person that has the ability to say: that was my fault, I could have done that better, I should have done that better.

In the reality, in this space with what people do, accidents happen. The really high-profile one was a tragedy where a young man fell of his bike, landed on his head and died in hospital two days later. That was front-page news, there was a coronial inquiry. We were exonerated. Every one of them presents an opportunity to learn; whether someone's died or whether you've got something wrong in an event. They are all opportunities to improve and be better and be more accountable and more responsible. You've got this massive responsibility to say, 'We do everything that we can within our power to mitigate the risk.'

You can never put on a risk-free event. And as we sit right now in these times of COVID-19, what we're trying to do is help our industry to come back. Our industry has been decimated globally.

Absolutely, there will be large portions, as in many industries, of our industry that just won't come back after this.

So, trying to work with event organisers, with governments, with stakeholders, to say: how can we come to an acceptable level of risk of putting on an event which minimises the amount of risk that we are exposing our staff to, our stakeholders to, our participants to? And that's always the rationale that we approach. We never know that we're going to stand on a stop line with zero risk, but we with a combination of all our stakeholders come to a level where we think we've got a plan to mitigate risk to an acceptable level.

DARREN: It's about balancing that. It's never going to get back to the way it was before, so where is it we can take it from where we are now to where we'd like to be. You talked about a review process. That after an event you go through the review process, can you explain to me what's involved in that? I think there's great learnings about how you review and the importance of doing it quickly after the event.

CHRIS ROBB: It's a great point, quickly is key. What we would do, and you can imagine on an event like that, your core team is probably working in most instances close to 48 hours with very little sleep. So, you're physically drained, emotionally drained, absolutely exhausted. What I would do is, typically the Singapore marathon is on a Sunday morning, most people won't finish until late Sunday afternoon and sometimes Sunday evening. And then the next morning is bringing the core team together, have a cup of coffee, start with a celebration. I'm always a fan of let's accept and acknowledge what we've done, and sometimes that gets derailed. You know, the debrief after the cycling event where the person died, that takes over the whole thing, you don't have the opportunity to celebrate. But the celebration – don't get carried away with the celebration. Like, we'll have other celebrations, but what could we do better? Whilst it's fresh in our mind, let's document it.

I used to have an expression that I would always start with: *egos at the door*. This is not a personal attack, but again overlaying what I shared with you in Asian cultures of making people lose face. You still need to be fairly open, in Australian culture you'd be able to say, 'Darren, you got that wrong.' You wouldn't take that approach to that degree in most Asian cultures. So it's respecting that, it's respecting people's boundaries, it's wording questions in such a way like, 'we had this particular issue here, how's the way that we might be able to resolve that in future?' as opposed to 'John, you didn't get that right, that created the problem'.

The Chris Robb Story

Chris Robb is the author of the book *Mass Participation Sports Events*, a highly sought-after International Speaker, High Impact Consultant and CEO of Mass Participation World. Chris's life reads like the pages of a novel. His amazing journey has allowed him to impact the lives of millions of people by creating and delivering mass participation sports events across three continents.

While there have been countless highlights, including working on the Sydney 2000 Olympics and meeting Sir Richard Branson at his home on Necker Island, Chris came from humble beginnings, growing up poor on a farm in Zimbabwe. Chris believes that our best chance to grow and learn often lies in times of extreme pressure. Along the way, he discovered events he initially perceived as 'disasters' were gifts. These significant moments taught Chris many valuable lessons that have helped him to be successful in business and to help others to achieve success.

His first business was started with a few thousand dollars, six months after emigrating to Australia. The business grew into a multi-million-dollar international company which was then sold to IRONMAN. He has been at the helm of some of the biggest mass participation events, including the Singapore Marathon, with 60,000 participants and 5000 staff and volunteers.

> **'If you can't stand the heat, you'd better get out of the kitchen.'**
> *Harry S. Truman*

Chapter 8

Excuses, blame and finger pointing

Many people are experts at assigning excuses, blame, finger-pointing or coming up with excuses for shortcomings in their life and career. It is more comfortable and less demanding to not take responsibility. Since it is always easy to play the victim and blame someone else or external circumstances for one's failings, not taking responsibility for yourself **and being held to account by others**.

Get ready folks because excuses, blame and finger pointing will gate crash your accountability party – they always do. Due, in large part to the fact that people seem to invite them to attend in the first instance. You see, people are experts at assigning excuses, blame, and finger-pointing for shortcomings in their life and career. It is more comfortable and less demanding than having to stand up and take responsibility, which is unquestionably the harder and far more challenging option.

Since it is always easy to play the victim card and to blame someone else or external circumstances for one's failings, taking responsibility for yourself and your performance gives you more control and greater choices, which I feel is the foundation of success in any endeavour.

As you'll read later in the chapter, I have faced many harsh obstacles particularly in the early days as a business owner. I think back to those dark days when the bank called in their loans and we lost our house to pay back mounting debt in excess of $500,000, and this was over 25 years ago – I could have blamed others, justified with excuses for my shortcomings as a business owner and finger pointed directly at others who I felt let me down, but NO ... not me ... that would be contrary to my values ... Instead, I looked at myself in the mirror, I wiped away the tears, and I vowed to take ownership for the failure and take control of my actions. In doing so, I took full responsibility for my role which led to the outcome, and pledged from that moment onwards in my life to make sure that this friggin nightmare NEVER happened again to my family or me. As a consequence, I got full accountability in place to guarantee that *'I do the things I say I'm going to do and get my team to do the same.'* I'm so lucky and truly grateful that in my lifetime I did get a second chance to do it better and do it all over again. There is real truth to the statement that what does not kill you makes you stronger.

'Conscientiousness' means *'the quality of being responsible, careful, diligent and taking responsibility for your actions and performance'*. All of these obstacles could have been valid excuses for me to give up and throw in the towel and play the victim card. I could have genuinely justified my businesses failure if I was to give it a post-mortem to help lessen my feelings and absorb the blow. Instead, I decided turn the tables around; I dug in deep to find my resilience and invited that to the party, which meant I brushed off the dirt, wiped my wounds, and I now proudly wear those scares as medals of honour in a fight that took me by the seat of my pants back onto the middle of the playing field so I could **play my best game.**

To get match fit, I quickly learnt and understood those elements that I got wrong or that I didn't pay enough attention to last time. Over many years, I have reflected on what I could have done better and got back on that horse as quickly as I could, and ensured that my history was never repeated.

All through my working life, I have taken elements from my last journey into my next. For me, it's like I always audition for my next career change during my previous entrepreneurial pursuits. I look back at my move to Apple, then got retrenched, to opening my own entrepreneurial marine and lifestyle business. Then after 15 years we sold that and exited to launch my Accountability Coaching practice called TICK THOSE BOXES, which is where I am today and loving every minute of it. Conscientiousness was the building block of my success.

Focusing on taking responsibility for what you can control is critical, and here's how you can start:

- ☑ **Value add:** Build your reputation and give more than you receive. If you are not adding value, go do something else.

- ☑ **Focus on what you can control:** Focus on taking responsibility for what you can control and not what you cannot.

- ☑ **Set and maintain the highest standards:** Set your bar high and continue to drive towards exceeding expectations, each and every time. Be empathetic, do unto others what you would like done to yourself. Then, add a bit more for good measure.

☑ **Be accountable:** You are responsible for things and accountable to people; do not ever forget that. Everyone needs Accountability Coaching because doing nothing costs you money and opportunity, and you're pissing people off with your lack of action.

☑ **Engage an Accountability Coach:** No, this is not a punishment for those who are lazy and lack business hunger, in fact it's absolutely the opposite. It's perfect for the high-performer who wants to **G**et **S**h!t **D**one, packing more into their days without having to work harder or longer. Forget doing nothing, that's called procrastination. Sticking your head in the sand and praying things will sort themselves out and improve, that's called hope.

HOPE is not a business strategy they teach at Harvard Business School. Steve Jobs didn't hope, he took action, and I played my role in that. For me, I'm about 'implementation and execution', everything else hinges on your ability to do this. I see this as critical for your business success.

If you WANT to get more done and juggle more balls in the air at any one time, you need to take action RIGHT NOW.

> **'You steadily grow into becoming your best as you choose to be accountable and accept responsibility for improvement.'**
> *Steve Shallenberger*

Be authentic – you can tell when it's not real

We live in a world of blame, watch the evening news nightly, and you will hear our leaders on both sides of the aisle blaming each other for interest rates, jobs, health care, and even football food prices. They will point the finger at the latest COVID hot spot and isolation breach, perhaps it's another untrained and PPE ignorant security guard having a smoko break with isolated hotel patrons. It's like there's a need to name and shame someone else. We want their picture to be mounted and framed on a wanted poster and circulated for all to see.

To own your life, you must take responsibility and that's what separates REAL reasons from the BS. That means there are NO excuses, there's NO blame and finger pointing is unacceptable behaviour which will not be tolerated in your organisation; regardless of its size. If you are a solopreneur, then this applies to you, just the same as if your team is 2,500 people like we learnt from Bruce Levy the former CEO of Medibank Private Health Insurance in chapter 2.

Excuses, blame and finger pointing is not real; it starts with you and good leaders set the standard for which others will follow. For those of you who are American history freaks, you know that President Harry S. Truman had a sign on his desk that read: 'The Buck Stops Here'. It meant he accepted full accountability for all the decisions of his administration. Truman's stand exists in organisations today but, unfortunately, as the exception rather than the rule.

When my children were little, they ran around the house, just like kids, and only stopped usually when they hurt themselves by accidentally running into a chair.

So, we played the **blame** the chair game. 'Ouch, that hurt,' they would scream. 'Why did you get in my way?' they would say to the chair.

'We're having so much fun, until you wrecked it,' they screamed, then they say to the chair 'that you spoiled it all for us'. Who do you think you are?

You are bigger and stronger... you hurt me. You're a bully.

And with that, we let our kids reach the seat to show it who was the boss. Obviously, it's so much simpler to blame the chair than to admit fault.

So, the kids continued to play and enjoy themselves.

Although you might be thinking this is a kid's game, a few people today continue to play the blame game as adults.

☑   'Don't blame me, I'm out of shape.'

☑   'It is not my fault that I have all this debt.'

☑   'I didn't know I had to finish the sales report by Monday.'

It's simple to blame the others

You have an option: you are able to blame havoc on the current weather, a terrible horoscope, or it's a leap year. Or you will get serious.

The simple truth is, when folks divert responsibility and throw **blame**, it functions as nothing more than a crutch and also a reason to quit trying.

Worse yet, individuals who always invent *excuses* why they cannot triumph to convince themselves that collapse is inevitable. This causes their fundamentally losing faith in their abilities and rendering it a self-fulfilling prophecy. So be careful how you speak to the others because you're probably listening too.

Powerful folks, those who achieve their goals, on the other hand, do not blame the world whenever they don't attain something. They accept personal obligation, they hold themselves to account and work with a partner to ensure full-accountability, and they learn from their mistakes, and then do something about it.

They also understand that being reluctant to make the effort required is like a losing match. In fact, those that state, 'I cannot' and 'I really don't wish to' activate the exact results.

It's important to see – even if you may well be making an endeavour today, matters might not be going your way. That's because you might well be paying a price for years of negligence. But that shouldn't deter you from making the effort today. The truth is it takes several years to become an overnight success.

The bottom line is, even if you'd like to achieve something in life, get to work.

Matters do not happen magically. YOU need to make things happen. Thus, be positive and be held to account. Stay focused with magnifying glass like focus and energy, to make fire with pinpoint accuracy and remain determined.

When you have a look into the mirror and do not like everything you see... do not blame the mirror and finger point.

Successful folks accept responsibility and are held to account by others because of their destiny; losers play the **blame** game; they make **excuses** and **finger point**.

I read that in 2014 the Brandon Hall Group's 'State of Performance Management Survey' a staggering 34% of global organisations said executives don't hold leaders accountable for performance. During the same year, results showed 39% planned to increase or significantly increase their focus next year on holding managers accountable. Finally, they are onto the road to accountability.

Without accountability, the most brilliant, hard-working, well-intentioned leaders in politics and in business will FAIL on numerous fronts. They will fail to meet their financial goals, they fail to develop their people and teams, they fail to hire and engage the best people and talent. They will also fail to coach and mentor their employees, they will fail to communicate and articulate clearly, they fail to optimise performance and seize opportunity, therefore they will fail the business. Effective leadership requires honest and continual accountability.

When leaders take personal accountability and full responsibility, that means the buck stops with them. Their implementation and execution of this is crucial which means they are willing to answer for the outcomes of their choices, their behaviours, and their actions in all situations in which they are involved. Accountable leaders don't blame others when things go pear-shaped.

Steve Jobs and my time at Apple taught me that accountable leaders must look to build a precise and accurate understanding of their entire organisation – from where it excels to where it seizes opportunity. Accountable leaders step up to champion opportunities to succeed. Accountable leaders always question the decisions and processes which shape their organisation. **Accountable leaders play their best game.** Accountable leaders ask well considered questions; they find answers, usually the best answers. Accountability goes beyond individual actions and decisions. Accountable leaders assume ownership for the performance of their teams – just like President Truman who assumed accountability for the performance of his administration from the day he took office.

An accountable leader takes responsibility. Remember you are responsible for things and accountable to people. Taking responsibility can be frightening, especially for new leaders. But it beats the alternative; having it forced upon you. Until you take responsibility, you are nothing more than a burden on your business and everyone around you who takes responsibly.

Accountability builds trust within teams, creates respect between leaders and employees, and promotes a sense of fairness that is essential to an engaged workforce. Accountability is about the near wins, not the wins. Accountability is in the striving and the reaching, the journey, the promise of getting there, and the perpetual self-refinement. Accountability is about a leader's commitment to excellence – elevating their game, keep improving and firing up. That is the mark of a true leader. Accountability is exactly why leadership is so tough and exactly why there are so few real leaders.

Are you accountable?

How have you gone about developing yourself to be more accountable? Consider what has worked and what hasn't as you embark on transforming your leadership culture to embrace accountability. How much of your success would you say is up to you, *your* choices, *your* actions, *your* behaviours vs. outside conditions?

I recently heard a simple but significant story that you may have heard before.

It is the story of four people called Everybody, Somebody, Anybody and Nobody. Here's the story, titled 'Whose Job Is It, Anyway?'

'This is a story about four people named Everybody, Somebody, Anybody and Nobody. There was an important task to be done, and everyone was sure that someone would do it. Anybody could have done it, but nobody did it. Somebody got angry about that, because it was everybody's job. Everybody thought anybody could do it, but nobody realised everybody wouldn't do it. It ended up everybody blamed somebody when nobody did what anybody could have'.

The story may be confusing, but the message is clear: no one took responsibility, so nothing got accomplished. It's that simple.

It is a story that often takes place in organisations and companies and teams, and everywhere there is a culture that lacks accountability.

The story could be summarised in any number of ways. It brings to life scenarios and phenomena that many people experience regularly:

- ☑ lack of accountability
- ☑ lack of ownership
- ☑ lack of responsibility
- ☑ finger pointing
- ☑ blame assigning.

All these components will not only have a negative impact on an organisation's ability to operate effectively, and on an individual's ability to do what he says, when he says it must be done, which involves embodying accountability.

These definitions are considered not complicated. Yet in practice, the outcome painted by the story appears far more common than not.

Over many years – perhaps since the beginning of time – organisational behaviour appears to have descended into chaos – with finger pointing and the apportioning of blame being far more prevalent than a clear understanding and execution of accountability and responsibility.

If a business has an aspiration to be sustainably customer centric, it can only be achieved with good governance – a plain and simple understanding of who does what – and when is an implementation of true accountability.

When it happens, they have a choice: they can lead with anger, frustration, blame, or they can take accountability, work with the team, engage to make sure that everyone from the top down does the things they say they will do, and they get their team members to do the same and solve the problem together.

The choice is yours, choose wisely.

I choose accountability and own my success in my work and in life.

When there's NO accountability, it all falls to bits ...

As I reflect on my business life, they are so many examples of where my best-laid plans have fallen apart through a direct lack of accountability and responsibility. Often caused by my own inability to recognise this at the time and to formulate corrections to my strategy.

For me age is a wonderful thing, which has given me permission to reflect openly and honestly and complete a post-mortem analysis of past events or circumstances that have led me to outcomes that perhaps could have and should have gone the other way in my favour if it was not due to insufficient organisational accountability, and personal responsibility demonstrated by me.

Let me share those emotional stories with you right now. In doing so, I'm needing to dig deep within and reopen my memory which has nicely protected some of this stuff because in parts, it still hurts. In doing so, I feel quite vulnerable, however I'm turning this to my advantage – as the wonderful Brené Brown says: 'Vulnerability is not winning or losing, it is having the courage to show up and be seen when we have no control over the outcome. Vulnerability is not weakness, it our greatest measure of courage' so here goes Brené I'm all in....

My first business

I got married at the ripe old age of 23, and am still proudly married today to Suzi for 35 years now and still happily and proudly counting. Back at the age of 27, our first child Jeremy was born and two years later we welcomed Adam into the world.

It was back in 1989 and during this time I founded a computer accessory and stationery business called Computer Office Supplies. We sold floppy disks, A3 continuous paper, magnetic tapes for mainframe computers, dot-matrix printer ink and acoustic covers; beautifully designed wooden boxes that would sit over a printer to reduce ambient noise. Nothing like the silent inkjet and laser printers of today. To give perspective, most items we sold were high volume consumables, meaning once finished they need to be regularly replaced.

Our average order value back then was $120 and an annual turnover was about $500,000, which means we processed over 4,000 orders a year or 76.9 orders per week.

The Australian Treasurer at the time was Paul Keating, and he famously described the 1990s recession as 'the recession we had to have'. And later he challenged Bob Hawke for the leadership of the Labour Party in 1991 and became Prime Minister of Australia.

The 'recession we had to have' was simply horrible. From the mid 1980s it was like a bubble swelling in size, which eventually burst. Interest rates were at record levels with crippling rates of between 19% and 24% if you were a borrower. And sadly, I was a borrower.

Can you imagine how this affected businesses of all kinds, because your interest bill was astronomical? When I look back, my business model was actually flawed right from the beginning, because my customers liked to buy from Computer Office Supplies due to the excellent quality of goods at competitive prices. Get more, pay less. I loved this...My service was underpinned by first-class delivery, which often exceeded customer expectations. When the goods were delivered an invoice was supplied, and it would be paid by their accounts payable team many weeks and months later. Danger and warning signs should have been flashing, but they were not, and I was oblivious, as I got on with my mission to SELL, SELL, SELL; just as Mr Turnbull would have liked. A simple recipe for success, so I thought ... but how wrong I was.

What I did not control was my finances; they were completely out of control. In fact, the growing number of debtors – those businesses who owed me money – was the first tell-tale sign which I overlooked but shouldn't have.

My business was being choked and suffocated by debt. It was my inadequate understanding of the economy and the direct connection between my growing overdraft and having to pay bank interest of 22% and by comparison, today's interest rates are circa 3.0%.

My average debtors' days exceeded 120, during a period of recession, which was some four months later when my tiny bill of $120 was paid. Yet in many cases, it was not paid and never would be. Which led to many failed attempts to collect the outstanding debt; it was unsuccessful, so we had no choice but to escalate the matter to our lawyer for collection. Whilst I still believe to this day this was the correct way to deal with this growing predicament, it was simply NOT cost effective for us to do so. I was effectively the supplier of computer accessories and of money. I was their bank, yet how unfair was it that I wasn't able to charge them interest like my bank was charging me at 22% for lending them money.

All this underpinned my tiny margins on the sale of goods, as I attempted to competitively grow the business and SELL more product to increase my revenue. Upon reflection, my business and the environment of the day was 'the perfect storm' as it blew my life and business apart.

Everything that was going on at the time seemed like a recipe for disaster for me, who was still pretty young and rather commercially naïve at the time. Suzi and I faced the bank-appointed administration and receivership head-on.

It was Christmas Eve that year when I laid off my entire team and closed the doors. It was a horrible Christmas. In the wash, we walked away with nothing. Suzi and I lost our house to the ANZ Bank. We were left with $500 in our account after attempting to pay our creditors. We lost our business and self-belief, then we said goodbye to such a lovely group of young people, my wonderful and trusting team whose Christmas and lives at the time were destroyed as well. Our debt was circa $500,000; no wonder we suffocated.

Then they say, if it doesn't rain, it pours... Nothing could be more accurate as shortly after that unforgettable Christmas we had a Great Dane puppy called 'Gus' which brought my young family so much pleasure and reward.

Dogs are amazing, all that unconditional love, so overjoyed to see you when you arrive home from work. Tongue out, tail wagging, just wanting to give you love, unconditional love and give you love in return. Gus looked like the cartoon character Scooby Doo. As a puppy Gus weighed 85kgs, and we loved him dearly with all our hearts, and during the collapse of the business, Gus was a welcoming and loving sight at the end of another emotional day dealing with all that mess in my business.

Sadly, Gus quickly became ill and he just wasn't himself. Lethargic, with a high temperature and no wagging tail – Gus was sick. We took Gus to the vet which soon became a regular visit with the diagnosis of heart disease. According to the Animal Health Centre, 'Great Danes are especially prone to a life-threatening heart condition known as dilated cardiomyopathy, or DCM, in which the heart becomes so large, thin, and weak that it can no longer effectively pump blood to the body.'

Later as a symptom of his illness and worsening condition, Gus developed severe incontinence. Imagine that, a Great Dane losing control; not a nice image at all. This was so heartbreaking, but also insanitary in our rented home. As the heart condition in Gus worsened, emergency surgery was required at a cost of $2,000.

Now let's understand what's going on here at this time; we had no home, no savings other than $500, and one of the positive things in our favour through this friggin train wreck of a time was Gus. And Gus is dying.

Thrust with having to reset our priorities which are aligned to our WHY and purpose which we discussed earlier was the easiest thing in the world. It was easy, so given no other option and saying no to the surgery was never going to happen, Suzi and I borrowed money from our family, yet again, and Gus got his surgery.

However, Gus never recovered from surgery and was put down a week later. What is going on here...

It's now some 30+ years later, and I often think about what would have been, what could have been, and what should have been if I only took on the responsibility of our financial health and took the necessary time to understand how it all worked in sync. Making the direct correlation between our sales margin and my debtors' days underpinned by the ridiculously high interest rates, meant that trying to grow my business like that was NOT good business. Doing business in this manner meant the more we sold, they larger our debt grew. That's not right, it should have been the opposite with our debt reducing as more sales were made. But, this can't happen if clients do not pay my invoices on time.

I was actually ruining my business, rather that growing it...

I often imagine and visualise 'What if?... what if I would have reduced debtors' days, what if it was COD only to support the cheapest prices on the planet? I know now that borrowings cannot sustain those substandard margins without having significant volume of continual sales to support it. And finally, what if I removed all that debt, because at 22% interest you simply can't borrow money...

Never did I use a spreadsheet, and we did have Lotus (acquired by Microsoft and the processor to Excel) back in the 1980s where I could model the business and give it a regular business heath-check to stay on top of those mission critical numbers.

I dare say, I've learnt my lessons well and there are no regrets because it's these life experiences, as costly and as emotionally draining as they may be, that have determined who I am and made Darren Finkelstein, The Accountability Guy® that's writing this today. Nowadays, I NEVER make decisions, regardless of the size, without first doing a spreadsheet to model, and better understand all those what if scenarios. Also, no more credit – I'm not your bank. If you want credit, then you ask your bank.

I read in a store recently: *'To god we give credit, all others pay cash'.* So, now for me and my businesses since the 1980s it's been bank transfer or credit card prior to being offered any of my goods or services. Lesson learned.

I know now that I could have written a different ending to this story rather than the sadness of administration and receivership. If I had done things differently and been held accountable for my decisions, had my finger on the pulse of my financial world and checked and analysed all the important numbers with regularity, it would have been an extraordinary ending indeed.

How I would have loved an Accountability Coach, Advisor and Mentor in my corner for my journey. Someone to work with me, hands on. So that I wasn't feeling alone and constantly out of my depth, with a monocular focus at the time.

Imagine if... back then I had someone who actually cared about my goals. Whose goal it was to help me reach my goal. Who was in my corner every step of the way! Imagine what I could have done if I had someone experienced in my corner; ready and able to assist, to support, to encourage me as the 27-year-old founder of Computer Office Supplies – the story would have had a completely different ending.

I accept that it wasn't meant to be... and as the business owner the buck stops with me. I was responsible for my insufficient accountability, and my lack of responsibility – demonstrated to my business and my people – let me down.

I was never held to account by myself nor anyone for that matter, until right at the end when it was too late and the bank wanted their money back, and they sold our house to get it.

At the time, I did not understand the fundamentals of running a sound business. This was underpinned by an insufficient recognition of the delicate and shaky period during *the recession we had to have*. Crucial to business success is many criteria that need to have a tick in those boxes.

Sadly, my boxes were crossed or left blank, yet I still pushed on and that cost me and my family dearly. These situations provide us with wonderful life lessons, and I look back at that time and take plenty of positive elements from that experience with me on my life's journey, which is still evolving.

Apple and BHP – The Big Australian

It was back in 1994, I was working for Apple as a Major Account Executive responsible for BHP, one of the largest Apple corporate customers and a valued member of the Apple Global Account Program at the time. BHP was the largest company in Australia during that time and one of the largest producers of steel in the world.

I found out later in the year that the Apple Executive Vice President, World Wide Sales and Marketing, would be visiting Australia, and I was to take him into BHP, our largest corporate account, for an executive briefing.

At the time, BHP had an installation of over 4,000 Apple Macintosh computers at their corporate headquarters at 600 Bourke St Melbourne and scattered right around the world. For me, this was fantastic as I saw it as a wonderful opportunity to grow my relationship with BHP, and calm the threat lurking in the wings from Microsoft, Apple's biggest opposition at the time. You see, 95% of the world were using a PC loaded with the loved Microsoft Windows Operating System and Microsoft Office suite of products.

In achieving that, this would set my position at Apple as a senior leader and someone who was critical to Apple's future success. I took this on as an opportunity to impress, and held a Major Account Planning Event (MAPE) meeting with the executive team from Apple Australia to plan the VP's visit and solidify the BHP account.

It was full on. I provided a bound strategy document for everyone in the room; it contained a SWOT analysis, it outlined all the players from BHP and their connection with Apple. I included an organisation chart on the stakeholders in BHP and how they rated our technology platform. We compared MacOS to PCs using Windows 86; it included the cost of ownership, support and repair costs, staff preferences, etc. It was so detailed and so informative that my Manager at the time was beside himself with excitement that his team had this under control, and we all were convinced our strategy was correct and positive about getting the outcomes we sought. We had a plan, a mighty good one indeed.

The executives from BHP had told us in the lead up that all the VP had to do was to confirm that Apple understands and appreciates BHP's case for using the Microsoft Office suite.

We would confirm that Apple would work closely with Microsoft to ensure that cross platform operability for BHP would be achieved … Simple enough. That strategy would work an absolute treat and the BHP team would be delighted with that outcome, or so I thought …

We picked up the VP from the airport in a limo (Americans love limos) and to my relief the VP pulled a copy of my MAPE document that I had created and presented (so beautifully, I might add) out of his bag, and said this was one of the finest documents he'd even seen. He went on to say that 'he wanted to get all the Apple sales teams on state side to do the same'. Yeah! Baby, that's my document – I beamed with pride. The VP had been sent a copy by the Apple Australia CEO, to review prior to the meeting.

In the car on the way the VP said it's all sorted, I got a fax from Bill today at Microsoft (Bill Gates that is) so I know exactly what I'm going to tell them. Phew! That's a relief, I thought, as we stepped out of the limo upon arrival at BHP in Bourke St with the VP, my boss and me.

Escorted by the executive concierge, we went straight up to level 35 in the executive lift (not the public ones) and directly to the BHP boardroom. We exchanged pleasantries and admired the view across Melbourne from high in the tower and sat down.

The coffee and appetisers were served by the executive hostess (yes, as it was called back then) never tasted so good. This is it, it's my time to shine.

I did my introduction, I talked about Microsoft and the importance to everyone of cooperation. I then passed the floor over to the VP to say the things exactly as he promised. A simple task, stick to the script the VP – you have one job to do. Positively address all the customer concerns with respect and empathy. Confirm how Apple Australia is supported by Apple HQ and Microsoft as we all work together to support the cross-platform environment that was BHP to run Microsoft Office on over 4,000 Apple Macintosh computers installed in BHP offices around the world. Exactly as outlined in my 'impressive' MAPE documentation.

The VP kicked back in his chair with an attaché on his lap; he opened it up to pull out a lengthy fax he'd received from Bill Gates and the Microsoft legal team only 24 hours earlier.

The VP said the fax was 'part of a legal case Apple had brought against Microsoft, which it countered, and that there would be NO sharing of technology'. The VP went on to add that he 'disliked Microsoft', and told Microsoft 'to f*off' that morning.

What the hell... YOU HAD ONE JOB TO DO!

That folks is the legendary story of how Apple lost the BHP account, with me at the wheel and responsible as the Major Account Executive.

Sadly, the VP was never held accountable; no-one would review his performance in quarterly or annual performance reviews. Upon reflection, it was obvious that NO responsibility was taken for actions on that day. All this underpinned the disregard for the agreed game plan, its implementation and execution. The loss of this corporate account worth around $2m to $5m per year, and I'm sure there's many others like it. The VP left Apple shortly after, leaving Apple's quarterly loss as significant, which adversely affected the share price and was diametrically opposed to where it is today, breaking corporate records with regularity.

Thankfully, I lasted way longer than the VP and experienced 10 years at Apple. I got a promotion shortly after, and in 1997 I became the 'Manager, Commercial Markets' which included: Major Accounts, Global Accounts, Retail, Apple Stores, Government, Publishing and Media, effectively everything other than education.

Even with the loss of the BHP account, my time at Apple was truly fantastic and profound indeed. Often, I felt like I was on the treadmill with the speed setting constantly being turned faster, and I was struggling to keep up without falling off, and running fiercely.

Fortunately, I never fell and flourished in the high-pressure ever-changing environment. Along the way I won the prestigious Golden Apple Award in 1998 received a unique 24ct gold Apple with a diamond inside as a gift. I'm always asked about Steve Jobs, who returned to Apple during my time as part of Apple's acquisition of the tech company NEXT whose operating system was the basis for the creation of the MacOS as we know it today. I'm always asked if I met Steve Jobs during my time. Yes, I had the pleasure of meeting the inspirational founder of Apple, and I trembled in my boots as he had a reputation for aggressively questioning employees he encountered.

I met Steve on a few occasions – he was god like. Everyone was in awe, everyone wanted to be like Steve, who could part a room just like the story of Moses parting the Red Sea in the bible. Steve would walk into a crowded space at Apple's HQ and the room would immediately part to make way for him. Steve was blessed with a unique ability to hold, engage and inspire an audience holding on to every single word he uttered. He would often share his dreams and visions which were always decades ahead of others.

That's my story – not bad at all for the high-school dropout who got to play with the cool kids in the BIG playground of Silicon Valley.

A wonderful experience which has truly shaped my view and my appreciation today, as I pride myself in taking ownership, and being fully responsibility for what I do. Holding myself to account and surrounding myself with others to hold me to account brings out the best in me and supports me to play my best game.

> **'For most people, blaming others is a subconscious mechanism for avoiding accountability. In reality, the only thing in your way is YOU.'**
> *Steve Maraboli*

Chapter 9

Where to from here?

If you like what you've read
in this book and would
like to work with me ...

Next steps ...

**IT ALL STARTS RIGHT HERE
RIGHT NOW...**

☑ Are you working hard but still not achieving your goals?

☑ Are you feeling overwhelmed?

☑ Do you need some direction on how to get your business to the next stage?

☑ Perhaps you are high-performing and successful and want to juggle more balls in the air at once?

☑ Accountability is your superpower that you must harness.

Before I get to the nitty-gritty, I want you to know that you're not alone.

I know what it's like to have all these ideas, but being unable to execute them. Or when you suspect there might be gaps and missed opportunities in your business, but you struggle to spot them, much less act on them.

I know what it's like to want to reach your goals faster, take on new projects and grow your business... but having nobody you can turn to for support, encouragement and to help you **G**et **S**h!t **D**one and to hold you to full accountability. This means *'you do the things you say you are going to do, and you get your team to do the same'.*

And I know how it feels when your goals feel more like dreams and desires...

... sometimes vague, sometimes specific, but always unmet and buried deep in that ever-growing to-do list.

Or when you feel so overwhelmed, it's overwhelming! What would you give to get on top of your business, instead of getting buried under it?

I know how to **G**et **S**h!t **D**one and get others to **G**et their **S**h!t **D**one too. I feel your pain in trying to run and grow your business.

There are so many moving parts to navigate. We want to get on top of our business but often, we just get buried under it.

The thought of launching or even managing a new project seems scary, because where do you even begin?

You begin here, right now, with me.

I'm about to offer you a lifeline. A proven way to define, achieve and surpass your business goals in the next 6 to 12 months and finally make those changes which are long overdue.

The answer is quite simple.

You need to *start setting realistic goals...*

... and start *being held accountable.*

You might have tried this in the past, but it didn't work out.

I'm going to show you why.

And I guarantee...

When you know how to become accountable, in the way I've outlined, the results will change your life and your business forever.

This new way of becoming accountable and making others accountable in your organisation is what separates successful business owners from those who spin their wheels, struggle to keep heads above water and throw in the towel.

When you know how to become truly accountable and introduce effective accountability training and systems to your organisation, you'll start to see your business go from strength to strength faster than you ever imagined.

... so you can finally start achieving more, move forward and put overwhelm in the rear view mirror.

My 'FREE' 15-minute ACCOUNTABILITY ASSESSMENT

Now you you've read my book, NOW it's time for you to take action, I can't ask for anything more from you right now...

Taking action is fantastic and a great start.

To ensure you take the first steps towards your road to accountability safe and slow, I'm extending to you a very special invitation.

Please join me privately for My 'FREE' 15-minute ACCOUNTABILITY ASSESSMENT.

PROCRASTINATION PARALYSIS?
IDEA OVERLOAD?
Boost Your Execution With My 15-Minute Accountability Power-Play

If you're an entrepreneur or business owner with more ideas than your current capacity to execute and implement, you might only be one strategy, tactic or tool away from turning those ideas in reality.

My 15-Minute Accountability Power-Play will reveal how accountable you really are...

During this fast-paced, speed-coaching session we'll...

1   Identify the ONE thing throttling your capacity to Get Sh!t Done.

2   Figure out what you must do first to throw that monkey off your back.

3   Plan what you must do next in order to get what you want.

To book, register here:
https://tickthoseboxes.com.au/accountability-assessment/

> ### 'Never promise more than you can perform.'
> *Publilius Syrus*

You have so much to gain, nothing to lose

There is NO downside for you whatsoever. If you do nothing, this is exactly the same as sticking your head in the sand. All this adds up to procrastination and hoping it will improve automatically – this does not help your situation. In fact, doing nothing always makes it worse.

You must take action now, otherwise tomorrow's result will be exactly the same as today. Implementation and execution are the key, and I'll ensure you follow the plan and you meet your deadlines. After all, that is what true accountability is all about.

Together, we can achieve your goals; you'll meet your commitments and promises that you've made to others and, most importantly, to yourself and you know you can't do it alone and get you to 100% on our road to accountability.

Maintaining your current status quo only means that you'll miss important opportunities to make money. You'll let people down, especially those that are important people to you, and that just pisses people off. Start your Accountability Assessment today!

So, let's get into this, there's a lot to do and there's no better time to take action than RIGHT NOW.

To book my FREE 15 minute ACCOUNTABILITY ASSESSMENT, please visit:
www.tickthoseboxes.com.au/accountability-assessment/

'To be accountable means that we are willing to be responsible to another person for our behaviour and it implies a level of submission to another's opinions and viewpoints.'
Wayde Goodall

Congratulations

You've now read **The Accountability Advantage – Play your best game**, so it's time for your graduation gift.

Download your free graduation **I GET SH!T DONE** wall poster in A3 (it's pictured on the next page) – this is a .pdf print-ready file for you to print, frame and hang proudly on your office wall.

I trust this serves as an important reminder of what can be achieved in getting to your 95% by following the road to accountability.

Hang it with pride, you deserve it.

With much gratitude and appreciation.

THE ACCOUNTABILITY GUY ®

The Accountability Guy®

Download from: www.tickthoseboxes.com.au/free-stuff/

215

DELIVERING WHAT YOU PROMISE AND GETTING YOUR TEAM TO DO THE SAME, IS WHAT ACCOUNTABILITY MEANS TO ME. DOING WHAT YOU SAY YOU ARE GOING TO DO IS CRITICAL IN BUSINESS. IMPLEMENTATION AND EXECUTION ARE KEY. I MEET DEADLINES, I KEEP PROMISES, I HONOUR COMMITMENTS I MAKE TO OTHERS AND TO MYSELF. ACCOUNTABILITY INCREASES MY OPPORTUNITY. I AM RESPONSIBLE, I AM LIABLE, I AM ANSWERABLE, I GET SHIT DONE. I SEE OPPORTUNITY, OPPORTUNITY IS WHERE I MAKE MONEY. I INCREASE MY EFFICIENCY BY LIFTING MY OUTPUT. ACCOUNTABILITY IS POWERFUL. OTHERS DONT KNOW WHAT IT MEANS BUT I DO. I UNDERSTAND WHY ACCOUNTABILITY IS IMPORTANT IN MY BUSINESS AND MY LIFE. I KNOW HOW TO CREATE A CULTURE OF ACCOUNTABILITY. OTHERS HOPE IT WILL HAPPEN, HOPE IS NO STRATEGY FOR ME, I REFUSE TO STICK MY HEAD IN THE SAND, I MAKE THINGS HAPPEN. I GET SHIT DONE. OTHERS HEAR THE A-WORD AND SHUDDER AT THE THOUGHT OF STEPPING UP AND BEING RESPONSIBLE FOR SOMETHING. I STEP UP, I NEVER SHY AWAY. I HAVE CLEAR FOCUS. I CREATE A PLAN, I SORT MY PRIORITIES AND CREATE SMALL MANAGEABLE TASKS. I STICK TO MY PLAN, I DELIVER. I UNDERSTAND THE DIFFERENCE BETWEEN ACCOUNTABILITY AND RESPONSIBILITY, THEY ARE COUSINS, BUT NOT THE SAME. I AM RESPONSIBLE FOR THINGS AND ACCOUNTABLE TO PEOPLE. DARREN FINKELSTEIN 'THE ACCOUNTABILITY GUY' HOLDS ME TO ACCOUNT WHICH IS ESSENTIAL FOR ME TO BE HIGH-PERFORMING. I LEAD BY EXAMPLE, I SET STANDARDS FOR MY TEAM AND OTHERS TO FOLLOW. I WISH OTHERS WERE HELD TO ACCOUNT, IT'S A BETTER USE OF TIME, WE'LL ALL MAKE MORE MONEY WITH LESS STRESS. I GET SHIT DONE. IT'S 2020 AND I PROUDLY **TICK THOSE BOXES**

I GET SH!T DONE

www.tickthoseboxes.com.au

WORK WITH ME PRIVATELY

– ATTENTION –

All high-performing Entrepreneurial Business Owners, Executives and Teams.

Are you juggling too many balls in the air at once, trying not to drop any of them? If so, that is a clue as to why you need me…

Accountability is my specialty; it's a tool that I've mastered for my business over many years. It held me in good stead at Apple, and it kept me ahead of the game in our business. The result is that I'm incredibly focused, well-organised and outcome-driven, which has led to my business success.

Yet for others, it frequently makes people nervous, as it requires us to step up our game, be introspective and hold ourselves to account, which can be very uncomfortable initially until you harness the superpower and momentum it generates, with the realisation how powerful it is, and how effective you have become.

Did you know that the word accountability is regularly misspelt and often misunderstood? Businesses don't really understand the difference between **responsibility** and **accountability**.

They are cousins but not the same. You see, you are **responsible for things** and **accountable to people**, hence the confusion.

To me, being **accountable** means '*doing the things you say you are going to do*', and '*getting your team to do the same*'.

Work with me directly and I'll keep you accountable, hold you to your commitments, promises and goals.

Turn Your Ideas And Wishes Into Reality With Accountability Made Easy

Accountability Coaching For High-Performing Goal-Kickers

How can The Accountability Guy® help you?

When you and/or your team are ready, take the following NEXT STEPS to ensure you become more accountable...

✓ **BOOK A FREE 15-MINUTE ACCOUNTABILIY ASSESS-MENT**
This is a fast-paced, speed-coaching session, facilitated by The Accountability Guy®, you will find out just how accountable you really are.

PROCRASTINATION PARALYSIS? IDEA OVERLOAD?
Boost Your Execution With My 15-Minute Accountability Power-Play

"If you're an entrepreneur or business owner with more ideas than your current capacity to execute and implement, you might only be one strategy, tactic or tool away from turning those ideas in reality."

My 15-Minute Accountability Power-Play will reveal how accountable you really are...

During this fast-paced, speed-coaching session we'll...

- ✓ Identify the ONE thing throttling your capacity to Get Sh!t Done
- ✓ Figure out what you must do first to throw that monkey off your back
- ✓ Plan what you must do next in order to get what you want

Book your session now
https://tickthoseboxes.com.au/accountability-assessment/

✓ **TAKE THE ACCOUNTABILITY SCORECARD QUIZ**
HOW ACCOUNTABLE ARE YOU? Discover your Accountability Score and increase the probability of smashing
your GOALS and Getting Sh!t Done!

WHY TAKE THE QUIZ?
(In case smashing your goals like pinatas with a baseball
bat isn't enough!)

✓ Answer 26 yes/no questions in under 4 minutes.
✓ Get a personalised report, tailored to you, with clear
   action steps.
✓ It's totally FREE – $0
✓ Accountability is a superpower

Take the scorecard QUIZ
https://www.theaccountabilityscorecard.com.au/

✓ **READ MY BOOK**
The Accountability Advantage – Play Your Best Game
Eliminate procrastination and overwhelm, and start playing your best game.

Buy a Copy
https://tickthoseboxes.com.au/theaccountabilityadvantage/

✓ **STUDY MY ONLINE COURSE: 'ACCOUNTABILITY MADE EASY'**
For high-performing goal-kickers who want to achieve even more success in work and in life. Enrol now and become accountable in a matter of hours.

Enrol NOW
https://www.accountabilitymadeeasy.com.au/

✓ **COMPLETE MY 30-DAY CHALLENGE**
Here's how to tick off any task on your To-Do List in the next 30 days (or sooner) without working harder, without letting anyone down and especially without giving up anything you love doing...

The **30-Day Accountability Challenge** will help you get it done so you can get on to the next exciting phase in your business or life.

The process is really simple...
1. First, I'll help you get CLARITY on what a successful outcome will look like
2. Next, you'll make it a PRIORITY by coupling your goal to why it really matters
3. Finally, we'll figure out what ACTIVITY needs to be done, when you will do it and who needs to be involved to make it possible

How much more time, money and opportunity are you going to waste by putting it off?

When in just a few weeks or days you could be enjoying the relief, satisfaction and pride of finally having it done.

All you need is a helping hand from the best accountability coach in the business...

Register NOW
https://tickthoseboxes.com.au/30daychallenge/

✓ **ONE-ON-ONE COACHING SESSIONS**
APPLY NOW for one of my private coaching programs; there are NO excuses because I have a plan for every ambition; let me show you how to stop missing deadlines and start Getting Sh!t Done.

Together, we'll start with my "Unboxing Session" so we can unpack everything you need to move forward with clarity on why smashing your goals, is so important to you.

Then, we'll have our weekly or monthly, private coaching sessions over Zoom:

Together we will:

1. Create a plan for achieving your goals, tasks and/or overcoming those roadblocks and obstacles.

2. Establish your priorities so that you know what needs to be done, the deadlines and due dates.

3. We will review your "To-Do List" and examine your implementation and execution together.

⇒ **Get Clarity**
Know what to do FIRST

⇒ **Get Started**
Know what to do NEXT

⇒ **Get Sh!T Done**
Know what to do MORE of

Check out my coaching packages
https://tickthoseboxes.com.au/coaching/

Are you a high-performing entrepreneur who wants to achieve more? Mastering accountability is your superpower.

Here's What To Do Next...

Step 1

Recognise that hiring an accountability coach is the secret to Getting Sh!t Done.

Step 2

Click BOOK A CALL to schedule your complimentary 15-minute "Accountability Assessment" with Darren.

Step 3

Choose the accountability package and plan that work best for you.

Step 4

Smash your goals like a baseball bat hitting a piñata.

Book your session now
https://tickthoseboxes.com.au/accountability-assessment/

Author Accountability

Ideal for those authors working with Andrew Griffiths or Michael Hanrahan at Publish Central only. I'll hold you to account to ensure you complete your manuscript on time. Hey, I've written four books, so I know how to plough through when it gets tough.

Custom and Bespoke Programs

Let's talk and I'll create a program specifically to meet your needs or the needs of your business. I've got a full playbook of strategies that I'm privileged to share, or maybe we can create a totally bespoke and customised package to suit your individual or team needs.

www.tickthoseboxes.com.au/working-with-me/

Speaker For Hire

Engage me to be a speaker at your next conference, webinar, event or workshop, either face to face or virtually.

I'll deliver engaging sessions online, or I can be on stage front and centre in person, whatever way works best for your event – I'm totally flexible.

It's about the audience taking action.

- ☑ I'll challenge thinking with my game-changing facts.
- ☑ Share my personal experiences… and a few Apple stories.
- ☑ Show the audience how to easily complete their goals and tasks on time.

www.tickthoseboxes.com.au/speaker/

DARREN FINKELSTEIN

Much more than a long surname...

For me, being The Accountability Guy® and business advisor means being able to present my ideas, share my experiences and tell my story with absolute authority. Getting the audience to take action is what I do. I deliver on stage or a virtual webinar with great passion and enthusiasm because 'I have walked the talk', these are all my experiences, not those of others.

My aim is to not only motivate, but to inspire people to 'implement and execute' what's needed right now in their businesses from this moment onwards. Implementing and executing is how you make money and achieving your goals, aspirations and dreams is how you'll live a fulfilling life.

Take a look at my key achievements in business, download my speaker kit and fill in the inquiry form on my website! Now it's time for you to take action.

Key achievements

- ☑ Ten years with Apple during the Steve Jobs era, 15 years in my own lifestyle entrepreneurial business which we successfully sold and exited confirms – 'I walk the talk'

- ☑ Radio 3AW Presenter 'Beach and Bay Reports'

- ☑ Dent Global: Australian 'Entrepreneur of the Year'

- ☑ Key Person of Influence by Dent Global, Featured Case Study (poster boy)

- ☑ 4 x Bestselling and Award-Winning Author

- ☑ iTunes Top 5 bestseller

- ☑ Apple iMac: Worldwide launch presentation team

- ☑ TV Presenter, All About Boats (Foxtel, Ch7 Mate)

- ☑ Ambassador 'Life's Better With A Boat'

- ☑ Golden Apple Award Winner – Apple Asia-Pacific

- ☑ Regular presenter at Andrew Griffiths' retreats and workshops (teaching other speakers and authors)
- ☑ Hosted Zoom webinars for 1,000 participants

Enquire Now

E: df@tickthoseboxes.com.au or call me now (+61) 418 379 369
W: www.TickThoseBoxes.com.au

Read my books

Honey, let's buy a BOAT!
Boat Ownership – Everything you wanted to know about buying (and selling) a powerboat but didn't know who to ask

Honey, let's go BOATING!
101 bucket list of boating destinations (Victorian edition)

Honey, let's sell the BOAT!
Finding the right buyer at the right price
– 9 practical tips –

www.tickthoseboxes.com.au/book-lists/my-books/

About me

G'day, I'm The Accountability Guy®, Darren Finkelstein. In case you didn't know, I'm an International Accountability Coach, Business Advisor, Mentor, Author, and Speaker.

I work with high-performing teams and people in Australia/New Zealand, the United Kingdom, the United States, Latin America, Europe, and Asia to assist them to achieve their highest goals and smash them like pinatas with baseball bats.

I accomplish this by drawing on over 30 years of expertise in the corporate and small business worlds.

Working with others

When working with high-performing entrepreneurial business owners, executives and teams, I ensure full accountability, so they meet obligations, goals, promises and commitments they have made to others and to themselves. This is critical when building successful businesses. Being passionate, energetic and focused. A leader who is accountable and driven; this is my life's journey, that's how I roll and that's how I play. I've got a full playbook to share, we'll implement and execute to ensure we meet the outcomes set. Furthermore, I also have a proven track record in both large corporate, big and small businesses which demonstrates that I deliver across all sizes and shapes of business.

I worked for Apple

For 10 years, I also worked for Apple as 'Manager of Commercial Markets' under the inspirational leadership of Steve Jobs (yes, I met him). During my time there, I won the prestigious 'Golden Apple Award' for the Asia-Pacific region. I regularly hosted senior executives and VIPs from Australian business to visit the Apple HQ in Cupertino, California, for technology tours and meetings with the Apple Executive team.

What an amazing experience for the degreeless, high-school dropout from suburban Doncaster in Melbourne, Australia to play on the biggest tech stage in the world, right in the heart of Silicon Valley. I often pinched myself to see if I was dreaming.

I got my sea change (genuinely)

So, after 10 years of incredible experiences and beautiful learnings from my time at Apple, along with a few battle scars, I was a genuine corporate escapee after getting retrenched from Apple, on the same day as those horrific terrorist attacks on the World Trade Center in New York, so I needed change, an actual 'sea change', which had always appealed to me. So, that is what I did!

Along with my business partner Andrew Rose, we created a boutique and entrepreneurial 'lifestyle business' in the marine industry. Our business started small, and then we snowballed to meet the needs of the market. Andrew and I then successfully sold the business and we exited some 15 years later to go off in our own directions.

My next challenge was as Marina Manager and Ambassador for Wyndham Harbour. This was a new residential, marina and harbour development for about 1,500 people (plus kids, dogs and boats) located on the north-western shores of Port Philip Bay in Melbourne's west.

Along the way during my time in the marine and lifestyle industry, I also wrote three award-winning bestselling books on boating, family and lifestyle. During this time, I developed 'The Boat Guy' as a brand and with that, I became a boating ambassador for The Boating Industry Association and industry expert, regularly presenting at Boat Shows and industry events. My first book – *Honey, let's buy a BOAT!!* – went Top 5 on iTunes. I built a strong community on social media, a growing media profile which is also widely respected within many entrepreneurial circles, where I'm known as the guy who constantly innovates, who doesn't stand still and who *Gets Sh!t Done*.

Naturally, this works for me. It's what I do and I'm very happy indeed to own it.

Along with promotional appearances, I became a seasonal presenter with radio 3AW (part of Macquarie Media and the Nine Network) where I present the 'Beach and Bay reports' over summer. I've done this professionally since 2014. I love the challenge of live radio, and this aligns well with my passion for the outdoors, lifestyle and the ocean, and enjoying life to the fullest.

If truth be known, I'm a wanna-be pro surfer with very little ability, but that's never stopped me.

Entrepreneur of the year

I graduated from the Dent Global 'Key Person of Influence' entrepreneurial accelerator program in 2012, where I was the first back-to-back winner of the 'Entrepreneur of the Year' award for Australia.

Enough about me, let's create your story together.

'You can't buy happiness, but Getting Sh!t Done is pretty much the same thing'.
Quote by Darren Finkelstein, The Accountability Guy®

My skills and experience

www.tickthoseboxes.com.au/about/

Skill Set: Here's what I bring to the table:

- ☑ Accountability Coach, Advisor & Mentor (2019 – present)
- ☑ Radio Presenter, Author & Speaker (2012 – present)
- ☑ Entrepreneur-In-Residence & Ambassador (2019)
- ☑ Marina Manager & Ambassador (2014 – 2018)
- ☑ Dealer Principal & Co-Founder (2002 – 2017)
- ☑ Manager Commercial Markets: Apple (1992 – 2002)
- ☑ Board & Advisory Appointments (current & past)

Let's keep in touch

If you want to connect with Darren Finkelstein, The Accountability Guy®, here's how:

Web
www.tickthoseboxes.com.au

Phone
Mobile: (+61) 418 379 369

Write
df@tickthoseboxes.com.au
P.O. Box 282
Caulfield Victoria 3162 Australia

Social Media

LinkedIn
Tick Those Boxes : www.linkedin.com/company/tickthoseboxes/

Darren Finkelstein: www.linkedin.com/in/darrenfinkelstein/

Facebook
Tick Those Boxes: www.facebook.com/TickThoseBoxes
Darren Finkelstein: www.facebook.com/darren.finkelstein/

Watch
YouTube channel:
www.youtube.com/channel/UCkoHvfRVEUcmV33-QS9XNyg

www.ingramcontent.com/pod-product-compliance
Lightning Source LLC
Chambersburg PA
CBHW040848210326
41597CB00029B/4772